Walking in the Footsteps of Robin Hood
in Nottinghamshire and Derbyshire

Jill Armitage

Published by Sigma Leisure – an imprint of
Sigma Press, Stobart House, Pontyclerc, Penybanc Road
Ammanford, Carmarthenshire SA18 3HP

British Library Cataloguing in Publication Data

A CIP record for this book is available from the British Library

ISBN: 978-1-85058-889-4

Typesetting and Design by: Sigma Press, Ammanford, Carms

Maps: © Bute Cartographics

Photographs: © Jill Armitage

Cover photographs: from top right, clockwise: Bronze statue previously housed at East Midland Designer Outlet, built on the site of the 12th century Pinxton Castle; Robin Hood's Cottage, Hathersage; Robin Hood's Stride; Bolsover Castle.

Printed by: Berforts Group Ltd

Disclaimer: The information in this book is given in good faith and is believed to be correct at the time of publication. Care should always be taken when walking in hill country. Where appropriate, attention has been drawn to matters of safety. The author and publisher cannot take responsibility for any accidents or injury incurred whilst following these walks. Only you can judge your own fitness, competence and experience. Do not rely solely on sketch maps for navigation: we strongly recommend the use of appropriate Ordnance Survey (or equivalent) maps.

Contents

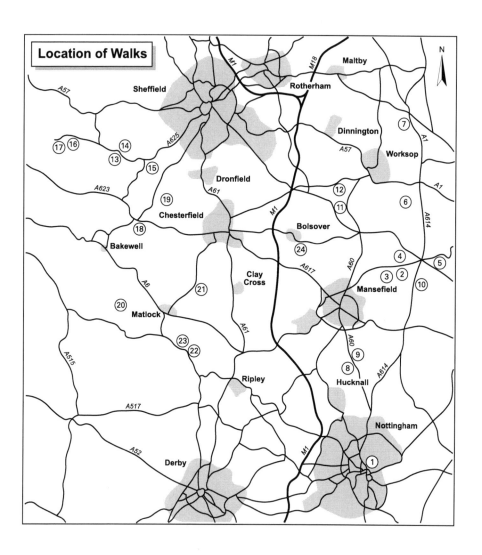

Introduction

On the borders of Nottinghamshire the county signs proudly proclaim that you are entering 'Robin Hood Country' and to many that means Sherwood Forest. By tradition, Robin Hood and his outlaws took refuge in these dense greenwoods, which in medieval times covered 100,000 acres, almost one fifth of Nottinghamshire and a large proportion of Derbyshire. It has now shrunk to a fraction of its former range but some sizeable fragments still remain. The most famous is the Sherwood Forest Country Park, near Edwinstowe. Yet, if you are approaching from the west you will have been travelling through Robin Hood Country for the best part of thirty miles, because the centre of the medieval Sherwood Forest was to the north of the town of Mansfield, now marked with a plaque known as the centre stone.

The Centre Stone

The everlasting popularity of Robin Hood and his exploits means that this is a magical area, known throughout the world, even by those who have never been near it, yet who was Robin Hood? Does the green-clad fugitive spring from popular folk tales rooted in pagan mythology, or were Robin and his followers of stubborn Saxon stock? I like to think that they were resistance fighters making a last stand against their Norman rulers, but over the centuries legend has become grafted on to fact, so we can never be sure. What we do know is that the legend of Robin Hood and the heroic tales of the Merrie Men remains Britain's most enduring and endearing folk tale.

Walking In the Footsteps of Robin Hood roots out the places mentioned in those old tales and visits the locations that Robin and his men would have known. We walk through some of middle England's finest countryside on miles of well-marked footpaths to interesting historical sites associated with the outlaw legend. We have traced stoops, caves, wells and stones with the outlaws names and woven them into our walks taking you through true Robin Hood country.

Walk 1: Nottingham
1½ miles (2.40km)

No book tracing the footsteps of Robin Hood would be complete without a walk round Nottingham. The suffix 'ham' meant village in the Saxon tongue but now Nottingham is a major city; the 7th largest urban area in the United Kingdom with a population of 667,000. The shire of Nottingham was created between the 9th-11th century, and Nottingham was granted its city charter as part of the Diamond Jubilee celebrations of Queen Victoria in 1897. It has been nicknamed Queen of the Midlands, and The Lace City but its most famous link is with Robin Hood, and his clash with the Sheriff of Nottingham.

In this walk around Nottingham City Centre, we try to find the romance and pageantry from a time before Nottingham's medieval heart was torn out, and its ancient castle complete with towers, and turrets and decaying dungeons was replaced by an 18th century build.

The Walk
Enter Nottingham on the A60 Mansfield Road (1) and you will pass York Street (2), where, behind York House, is the only surviving reminder of the ancient King's Great Highway. Robin Hood purportedly hid or stabled his horses on the site of York Street, in order to make a fast get-away.

Shire towns such as Nottingham had a defensive wall around them and, as you pass the Victorian Shopping Centre and enter the city of Nottingham, you are about to cross Upper Parliament Street (3), which is where the town walls once ran. Part of the wall, originally thirty feet high and seven feet thick, was discovered here when the railway was being laid through Nottingham. It's now in the castle grounds.

Continue down Clumber Street until reaching the Council House, Exchange Building and Arcade (4), built by Cecil Howitt in 1920 in classical style. Note the impressive domed cupola, then go inside, locate the cupola and look up. It's 200ft high under the dome which is 28ft in diameter.

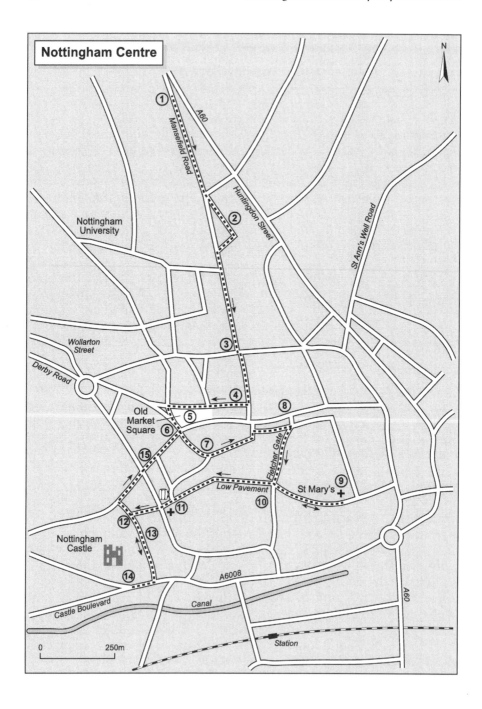

In each of the four spandrels, you'll see impressive frescos (paintings done directly onto plaster) by two local artists Noel Denholm Davis and Hammersley Ball. Each fresco marks a great event in Nottingham's history; the Danes capturing the town, William the Conqueror ordering a castle to be built, Charles I raising his standard at the start of the Civil War, and Robin Hood with his outlaw gang.

To get Robin's stance as a bowman correct, the artist took archery lessons. He modelled the figures on local celebrities and borrowed the faces of Albert Iremonger, the 6ft 4ins goal-keeper of Notts County Football Club for Little John and Mrs Popham, wife of a local doctor for Maid Marion.

While here, you might hear the chime of the hour bell of the nine foot clock, hung 200ft (61m) up in the dome of the adjoining Council House. It is one of the loudest and deepest toned (E-flat) bells in Britain, and on a good day it can be heard seven miles away. It has a similar tone to London's Big Ben, but this is Nottingham, so this ten-ton bell is named Little John.

Wander outside into The Old Market Square (5) , the heart of the city. This was originally the town green where the Sheriff held those famous archery contests. Robin would have competed here on many occasions. Those early fairs were the predecessor of St Matthew's Fair, held annually on 27th September, later renamed The Nottingham Goose Fair and moved to the Forest Recreation Ground, where it is still held today.

In 1155, King Henry ll granted Nottingham a charter to hold a twice-weekly market in the Market Square, and it was here that Robin, disguised as a potter, sold his pots and, disguised as a butcher, sold his meat.

On the west side of the Market Square is Beastmarket Hill (6).

Here stands The Bell Inn, one of the three contenders for the title of the oldest inn in Nottingham. It is believed that The Bell Inn was built around the refectory of an old Carmelite Friary that could possibly have been the original home of Friar Tuck. Because of its religious connection, the original inn was called The Angel. The main passageway has the original flag-stones along which travellers led their horses to the stables at the rear of the building The cellars date from Norman times, with a small cave reputed to be Anglo-Saxon.

From Beastmarket Hill go down Wheeler Gate, passing St Peter's Church (7), which probably dates from around 1180, then wander between the courtyards along St Peter's Gate, crossing Bridlesmith Gate and along Bottle Lane until reaching Fletcher Gate (8).

Fletcher Gate is now a main thoroughfare running north from the Broadmarsh Centre, yet it still retains its name from the days when this street housed the workshops of the Bowyers(bowmakers) and Fletchers (arrow makers). Tradesmen built their workshops at the front of the building where they and their families lived.

The wood to make an arrow would need to combine strength and lightness, and black poplar wood was especially good. Each shaft or stele would be between 27-35 inches. One end held the flights made of goose (or peacock feathers for the rich), stuck on with pitch and tied with silk or linen thread. The other end had an iron arrowhead made by the local blacksmith, attached with a glue made out of bluebell bulbs.

Our next location is St Mary's Church (9), where Robin went to pray in the ballad *Robin Hood and The Monk.*

In AD500 the Saxons arrived and decided to build their settlement where St Mary's church now stands. The Saxon church was recorded in the Domesday Book of 1086, incorporated into the Norman church, which was built in 1474, giving us the late medieval building you see today as you enter the world-renowned Lace Market area.

In the original ballad, Robin was very restless and came to St Mary's Church in Nottingham, where he was recognised by a monk he had formerly robbed of one hundred pounds. The monk alerted the sheriff, Robin was captured and thrown into the dungeon under Nottingham castle, and the monk rode to London to get an execution warrant from the King. But help was at hand. The monk was waylaid and replaced by Little John who obtained the warrant and returned to Nottingham castle. The sheriff declared a celebration, got roaring drunk and passed out, giving Little John the opportunity to slip down into the dungeons and rescue Robin.

But just suppose that this was done with the help of the sheriff's wife. What if the reason for Robin's restlessness was because he was planning an assignation with his lover! If she had been late for her appointment and arrived as Robin was being arrested, she could have ridden into Sherwood forest on that little white horse he gave her in 'Robin Hood and the Potter', to raise the alarm. She could have made sure that Robin's incarceration in the castle was made more bearable, and at the celebratory feast, drugged her husband's wine to give Little John the opportunity to release her lover.

Let's follow in the footsteps of Robin Hood, who was dragged from St Mary's Church to Nottingham Castle, so cross Fletcher Gate (10), go down Low Pavement and turn left into Castle Gate, one of the four medieval streets which ran from the castle to the market place. Continue to the end of this section of Castle Gate where it meets Maid Marion Way and on your left is St Nicholas' Church (11). The present building was constructed in 1671 on the site of a very much earlier church, founded about the time of the Norman conquest (1066). Robin Hood is said to have used St Nicholas' as a hide-out.

On the opposite side of Castle Gate is Ye Olde Salutation Inn built circa 1240. It got its name from the Annunciation of the birth of Christ by the Angel Gabriel to the Virgin Mary and is also known as 'Archangel Gabriel Salute the Virgin Mary'. It may have originally been the guest house for the Carmelite or White Friars on Beastmarket Hill. The building is ancient, but the cave system underneath was in existence long before a building was ever

Robin would have competed in the archery competitions in the Old Market Square (statue outside Nottingham Castle)

thought of. Here, the cave's design and construction, with a 70ft well sunk through the rock, would have been an ideal spot for an early cave settlement. In 868AD, Asser, bio-grapher of Alfred the Great wrote of Nottingham being called 'Tigguocobanc' or 'House of Caves'. Most of Nottingham lies on soft, Bunter sandstone, sedimentary rock laid down millions of years ago and going down to two hundred feet. Generations of troglodytes have scooped them-selves homes in it. It's surprising that there is no mention of Robin taking his mattock, shovel and mallet and digging himself a town house, but perhaps that would have been too close for comfort to his arch-enemy at the castle.

The statue of Friar Tuck outside Nottingham Castle

In 1336, when Edward III stayed at Nottingham castle, many of his retinue were quartered and fed at 'Ye House By Ye Sign of Salutation.' In 1642, when Charles I raised his standard at Nottingham, the inn was used as a recruiting office and, during the coaching days, the house had a sinister reputation, as it was frequented by highwaymen.

Cross Maid Marion Way, described as the ugliest road in Europe and an insult to Maid Marion, and resume your journey on the other section of Castle Gate. This was once the red light district, but we'll not go there.

Straight ahead is Nottingham Castle and the dry outer moat, where in pride of place now stands the seven-foot effigy of Robin Hood (12), sculpted by James Woodford and presented to the city by Philip Clay, a local businessman to commemorate the visit of Princess Elizabeth and the Duke of Edinburgh on 28th June, 1949, during the city's quincentenary celebrations.

Robin is cast in eight pieces of half-inch thick bronze, weighs half a ton and stands on a base weighing two and a half tons. Compared to our modern day superheroes who are tall, slim and fit, this figure is rather short and stout, which has earned it the nick-named 'the world's largest gnome'.

This area is a very popular tourist attraction and no self respecting visitor would leave without having their photograph taken with Robin as he sturdily draws an invisible bowstring. Unfortunately, our medieval outlaw is no match against twenty first century vandals and souvenir hunters, and without his bow string and arrow, poor Robin stands there in a strange boxing stance, so a bit of imagination is needed.

Bronze plaques depicting events in the legends of Robin Hood are set into the castle walls around this area. The four reliefs show Maid Marian helping Robin and Friar Tuck in their fight against Guy of Gisbourne's men; King Richard the Lionheart joining Marion's hand with that of Robin; Robin and Little John fighting on the bridge, and Robin shooting his last arrow.

Dotted around are reclining figures of some of the major figures in the outlaw band – Little John is repairing his bow, Friar Tuck is reading, Will Stutely is reclining, and Allen a Dale plays a harp to Will Scarlet.

Turn round and across the road you will see a remarkable medieval merchant's house dating from 1450 (13).

It's original address was 10 Middle Pavement, but the building was moved to this site 'en bloc' when the Broad Marsh Centre was built in 1969. In its original position it was a restaurant known as The

Bronze placque showing Richard the Lionheart, Marion and Robin

The Severn Building, a medieval merchant's house

House of Severn, now it is the Lace Centre, devoted to the history and sale of the world famous Nottingham lace, where demonstrations of hand-made lace making are still shown.

Walk down the hill to The Tryppe to Jerusalem Inn (14), hewn out of the rocks beneath Nottingham Castle.

The Tryppe, an Old English word for halt or gathering place, was built in 1189, the year of the ascension of King Richard the Lionheart. He crusaded against the Saracens who at the time occupied the Holy Land, so it's possible that this inn would have been a watering hole for knight's going to the Crusades. It's also reputedly the oldest inn in England, although in Nottingham alone it shares that distinction with The Bell and Ye Olde Salutation Inn. The Tryppe was originally the brew house for the castle and there is still the remains of a speaking tube between there and the castle.

Robin Hood may have indulged here too, so can you visualise it as it was then? This tavern would have been a hot-bed of gossip and the customers would have been entertained by a ragged minstrel who wandered round fairs, markets, wayside inns and anywhere he could attract a paying audience. In order to get the attention of the audience, he'd start with something like the opening lines of 'The Lytell Geste of Robin Hood'.

> *Lythe and listen gentlemen that be of frebore blode*
> *I shall you tell of a gode yeoman, his name was Robyn Hode*

Just below the castle is Fishpond Drive, running parallel to Castle Boulevard.

In Norman times, this area was honeycombed with caves that were the homes of an important group of religious hermits.

Nottingham Castle stands on it's 133ft rock, although anything less castle-like is hard to imagine. What happened to that chunky, impregnable stone castle that the name conjures up, the fortress built in 1068 by William Peveril on the instructions of William the Conqueror? The original castle would have been a wooden structure on top of the same high crags, surrounded by a palisade of wooden stakes and a moat. Curling round its base to the South was the River Leem, diverted by the Normans and diverted again to flow into the Nottingham and Beeston canal, when the Castle Boulevard was constructed more recently.

In the time of Robin Hood the castle was one of Prince John's headquarters and, in 1170, Henry II gave money for the building of a stone castle to replace the old wood and earth structure. This early medieval castle was destroyed during the Civil War, so that was the end of the mighty fortress that had over-awed the Midlands for 600 years. In it's place, in 1679, this Palladian style palace was built by William Cavendish for the sum of £14,000, at the same time that he was building Bolsover Castle (see walk 24). Incensed rioters set it ablaze in 1831; it lay

An artist's impression of what Nottingham Castle would have looked like in the days of Robin Hood

The Gate House of Nottingham Castle

in disuse for forty years but was then restored in 1875, when the corporation acquired the lease. The Oxford University Trust acquired the building, which was sold in 1952 to the city of Nottingham for £16,000.

Emrys Bryson in his book 'Portrait of Nottingham' suggests selling it the Americans and replacing it with a proper castle that lives up to the expectations of the thousands of disappointed visitors that flock to see the stump of a romantic castle complete with towers and turrets and decaying dungeons.

Pass through the great stone arch of the restored, but feasibly ancient, gatehouse where the rattling chains of the portcullis once clanged and a drawbridge creaked ominously beneath the weight of heavily armoured knights. It's almost possible to imagine the clink of swords as the knights charge out of the guard rooms, but now this houses a souvenir shop and a display about Robin Hood and his men. Walk up to the castle where, since 1965, a collection of artefacts of the Worcestershire and Sherwood Forester's Regiment has been housed. Recent excavation work has uncovered parts of the original castle that are now open to the public and it is possible to go on a guided tour of the castle's tunnels and caves that honeycomb the rock on which it stands. These caves were used as dungeons where many prisoners were incarcerated. In 'Robin Hood and the Monk', Robin was captured and thrown into the dungeons under Nottingham castle, but Robin Hood escaped from his captivity.

Leave the castle and walk along Friar Gate. Cross Maid Marion Way (15) and continue ahead until reaching the Old Market Square in the very heart of Nottingham.

Walk 2: Sherwood Forest – Major Oak – Archway House – Edwinstowe

Distance	4½ miles (7.30km)
Starting point	Edwinstowe
How to get there	Take the A6075 from Mansfield to Edwinstowe. Turn left at the cross roads along the B6034, and half a mile later turn into the Sherwood Forest Visitor Centre Car Park
Parking	The Sherwood Forest Visitor Centre Car Park. There is a parking fee but the facilities at the visitor centre are excellent
Map	Ordnance Survey OS Explorer 270
Map reference	GR 627676

Sherwood Forest with its ancient woodlands, giant oaks and outlaw legends has a unique appeal for the visitor in general and the walker in particular. This is the conventional walk through Sherwood Forest, Robin's favourite hide-out and home, to the ancient Major Oak, but we extend it to pass Archway House, a folly that displays all the major Robin Hood characters in elevated niches around the walls, before returning to Edwinstowe, the village in the heart of Sherwood Forest that has an unparalleled association with the Robin Hood Legend.

Statue of Robin Hood at the Visitor Centre

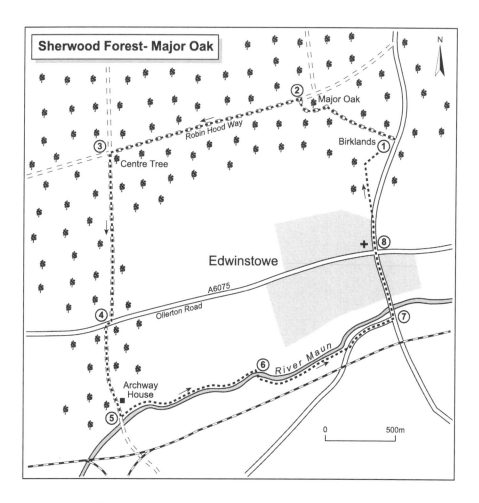

The Robin Hood Connection

In Robin Hood's day, Sherwood Forest was an unbroken woodland that covered 100,000 acres; almost one fifth of Nottinghamshire a large portion of Derbyshire and the lower band of South Yorkshire. This was a royal hunting forest, its valuable game, timber, cattle and land protected by strict forest laws. Here, the Norman aristocracy enjoyed the exclusive privilege of the chase, while the villagers scratched a living from the dry, sandy Sherwood soil. Against this background of unrest and inequality, in the forest theatre of Sherwood, the stage was set for the appearance of the celebrated Robin Hood and his companions to perform their own kind of forest rule. As you enjoy your walk, watch out for honourable thieves in these leafy glades, relieving rich nobles of their purses for more equitable distribution.

The Walk

Leave the car park (1) and follow the route signs to the Visitor Centre. All three colour coded walks start from here. The shortest route is to the Major Oak, denoted by blue banded posts. This path is surfaced and suitable for wheelchairs and pushchairs. To take this route – as everyone does – bear left directly in front of the visitor centre. Ignore the Greenwood Walk – denoted by green banded posts a few yards later, and follow the fenced, gravel path until it forks, then keep following the signs for the Major Oak. Cross a public bridleway, where there's a sign telling you that the Major Oak is five minutes walk away. As you pass the many stag headed and sculptured old trees, you can almost feel the tension building.

The Major Oak
This mighty oak is one of the landmarks of Sherwood Forest and has fascinated visitors since tourists discovered Sherwood in Victorian

The Major Oak

days. Then, and up to 40 years ago, you could climb all over it, but not now, so when you reach the Major Oak, don't be disappointed that you can't enter or even get within ten feet as the whole is surrounded by a wooden fence. Estimated to be between 800-1,500 years old, this portly old specimen, with its 35ft girth, 52ft height and 92ft spread now needs a lot of support.

Its arthritic limbs are patched with lead sheet and propped with iron shackles, yet every year it sprouts new growth and a fresh supply of acorns. It is one of the oldest and largest trees in England. In case you are wondering why it's not called Robin Hood's tree, it's named after Major Hayman Rooke, a noted historian who, in 1790, first described the tree in his publication 'Remarkable Oaks in the Welbeck Estate'.

Continue round the fencing that surrounds the tree until you encounter the green bow and arrow direction signs that denote the

Archway House

Robin Hood Way (2). Follow the direction of the arrow by turning left along a gravel path and stay on this until reaching the meeting point of six tracks. Ignore the one on your immediate right and take the second one, the wider bridle path. The route takes you past the heath land, then on through an old oak plantation.

Ignoring all minor paths, after half a mile, fork left, then at a point where a number of paths converge, keep forward to reach a stony path, then turn left to follow another bridleway. Remain on this track for 1½ miles passing the Centre Tree (3), and just before reaching the A6075 (4), bear right along the bridleway running parallel with the road on your left.

After a short distance, cross the road and take the bridleway opposite to Clipstone. This is Archway Road and you are following the Robin Hood Way again. After a few hundred yards you'll arrive at Archway House.

This is one of the most unusual and impressive buildings you are likely to encounter, and you will not be surprised to learn that it was built as a picturesque folly in 1842 by the Duke of Portland. It's Gothic in character with buttressed walls and traceried windows on each side of a central arch. The façade is decorated with carvings of forest life and set in niches in the north side are statues of Friar Tuck, King Richard I and Allen a Dale. In niches on the south side are statues of Robin Hood in Saxon dress, Little John and Maid Marion. Archway house was once a school but is now a private residence.

After passing Archway House you will encounter a bridge over the River Maun, but just before it is a footpath on your left (5). Follow this path with the river on your right until reaching an agricultural bridge across the river (6). Cross to the other side and continue with the river on your left for nearly half a mile until reaching a surfaced road. Follow this to the main B6034 road (7) and walk straight through Edwinstowe.

The village was named after Edwin, the first Christian King of Northumbria, who died at the battle of Hatfield (or Heathfield) in 632, in the fight between the pagans of Mercia and the Christians of Northumbria. His men gave him a secret burial in the forest clearing

The statue of Robin and Marion in the centre of Edwinstowe

and a small chapel was built on the spot (see walk 4). The word Stowe means the holy or burial place - thus Edwinstowe.

As you pass through the village, pause to admire the life size bronze statue of Robin and Marion outside the library, unveiled in July 1998.

Proceed to the cross roads in the centre of Edwinstowe (8), the junction of Mansfield Road (A6075) and Church Street GR 625669, and go straight ahead, passing the church on your left.

St Mary's Church is said to be the place where Robin Hood and Maid Marion were betrothed. A sign in the churchyard even notes the supposed wedding. St Mary's Edwinstowe is an impressive 12th century church. Attractions include a beautiful parish tapestry, the carved stone heads of Archbishop Thomas Becket and King Henry II, a mysterious face in the stained glass east window and a 'Forest Measure', set into the wall to the left of the memorial to the Rigley and Ward families. This is believed to be an ancient rule for measuring land.

At the edge of the village, turn left at Forest Corner, then immediately right following the track which runs along the side of the cricket ground. At the far side of this, follow the sign for the Visitor Centre and the Major Oak to return to the car park which is the start/end of this walk.

Walk 3:
Clipstone and King John's Palace

This walk takes us from New Clipstone to Old Clipstone, which is still marked on maps, although this area had a name change to King's Clipstone a few years ago in recognition of the former royal hunting lodge known as King John's Palace.

We start and end our walk at Vicar Water Country Park, created on the site of former spoil heaps from Clipstone colliery, where you'll find a visitor centre and a café.

Distance	6 miles (9.70km)
Starting point	New Clipstone
How to get there	Take the B6030 from Mansfield and after 2½ miles you will reach a roundabout on the outskirts of Clipstone. After 500m, take a road on your right and follow it round to Vicar Water
Parking	Vicar Water Car Park off the B6030 at New Clipstone
Map	Ordnance Survey OS Explorer 270
Map reference	GR 587627

The Robin Hood Connection

Here is the palace where King John would have entertained many rich and powerful nobles, who provided rich pickings for Robin and his gang. It's also possible that when they ambushed one particularly wealthy cavalcade on their way to Clipstone, amongst the party was Lady Marion. Could Robin have carried her off into the greenwood intending to claim a ransom for her safe return? After some dalliance

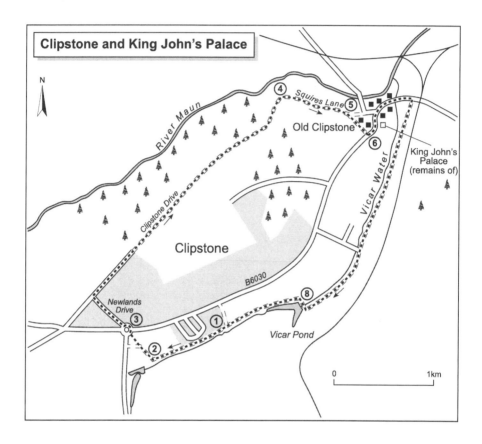

she was returned, but in the meantime she had lost her heart to that dashing young outlaw, and the feeling was mutual.

The Walk

From the car park (1) turn right in front of a pond to join a clear track. Turn right at a signpost next to the Bridleways Guest House and holiday homes (2) and follow the road to the roundabout on the B6030 (3). Cross the road and continue in the same direction along Newlands Drive until reaching the T-junction with Clipstone Drive. Turn right and continue for 1½ miles with houses on your right, then later fields. Ignore all side turnings, eventually reaching Cavendish Lodge (4). In front of the lodge, the track bends to the right and becomes a surfaced lane – Squires Lane. At the fork (5), branch right and continue until reaching the main road at King's Clipstone (6). Turn left and walk along the road. The ruins of King John's Palace (GR 603647) are over on your right behind the houses in the field, which is private.

The scanty remains of King John's Palace stand half forgotten in the middle of a hay field. It was built originally as a church by King Edwin, the first Christian king of Northumbria, and dramatically extended later by Henry I into the building that King John would have known. It was used as a hunting lodge by every English King that visited Sherwood to hunt the Royal deer, and provided stabling for over two hundred horses.

Following a fire, a lot of building work was done under Henry III. Edward I was probably staying at King John's Palace when he called a Parliament to meet at the nearby Parliament Oak, and his son Edward II frequently came here for the sport. Its decline started near the

The ruined King John's Palace

beginning of the reign of Henry IV when the king gave the lodge to the Earl of March in recognition of his loyalty. The lodge was ruinous by 1525 and further damage was done to it during the Civil War.

Continue along the road until reaching the Dog and Duck public house on your right (7). Walk into the car park by a signpost. From here there is a clear view of the ruins over in the field on your right. Continue diagonally across the car park to join a rough track running parallel to the railway line for just over 1¼ miles, with Vicar Water on your right and the railway line on your left. Pass under two bridges before reaching Vicar Pond (8). Turn right and follow the lane round the pond. Go through a long tunnel and at a junction turn right to reach the car park and the start/end of this walk.

king John would have entertained lavishly at his Palace in Clipstone (H. Pyle)

Walk 4: Edwin's 'Stowe' or Burial Ground – Edwinstowe

This, our second walk through Sherwood Forest, gives us the opportunity to see more of the area and the site of the 7th century chapel that marked St. Edwin's 'stowe' or burial ground, from which the current village gets its name.

Edwin was the first Christian King of Northumbria, a land which in the 7th century stretching from the River Trent in south Derbyshire to Edinburgh in Scotland. Encouraged by the persuasive powers of his wife Princess Ethelburga of Kent, Edwin was converted to Christianity by Bishop Paulinus, and along with many members of his court, was baptised on Easter Sunday, 625AD in a small church in York – later to be rebuilt as York Minster. The site is now marked in the crypt of the Minster, but Edwinstowe was Edwin's last resting place. The word 'stowe' means the holy or burial place.

Distance	7¼ miles (11.75km)
Starting point	Forest Corner, Edwinstowe
How to get there	Take the A6075 from Mansfield to Edwinstowe. Turn left at the cross roads along the B6034, passing the church and after 250m turn left into the car park. If in doubt follow the signs for the YHA, which is next door
Parking	The Sherwood Forest Art and Craft Centre Car Park
Map	Ordnance Survey OS Explorer 270
Map reference	GR 624672

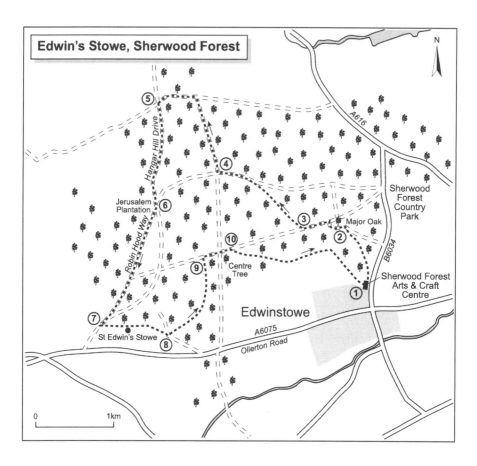

Edwin had encouraged Bishop Paulinus's missionary activities in Northern England, and Northumbria became the first Christian kingdom in the country. To honour his fight against the ungodly, Edwin was canonised and became Saint Edwin.

The Robin Hood connection

The chapel marking Edwin's burial place was in existence in King John's time, because there is a record that John paid a hermit to live there and pray for his soul and the souls of those he had wronged. There's every possibility that Robin and his men could have worshipped there. For centuries this chapel was associated with the royal chapel at Clipstone Palace 1½ miles away, and as a chantry chapel it came under Henry VIII's ban, and was allowed to fall into ruins.

The Walk

Leave the car park (1) and head for the cricket ground on your left, take the path around the right hand side of the pitch.

Between Easter and October there's a fun fair near the cricket pitch – a great distraction for the children. There's been an annual fair in Edwinstowe since 1381 when a Royal Charter granted this yearly event to be held on the saint day of St Edwin – October 24th.

Near the entrance are two boards with painted pictures of Robin Hood and Maid Marion with holes cut out for you to place your face for a photo opportunity.

At a fork turn right to leave the cricket ground and shortly afterwards turn right again at a crossroads. This path leads to the visitor centre from where you follow the signs to Major Oak (2). Take the second left. At a crossroad of paths (3), turn right to temporarily leave the Robin Hood Way onto a public bridleway. Keep on the brideway and continue ahead where it crosses a public footpath. At a T-junction, turn left then immediately right at a crossing of tracks entering the Dukeries Training area (4). This track rejoins the Robin Hood Way.

Keep ahead on the clear track with the woodland on your left and an open area of your right. Ignore all side turns until you reach a crossroad of paths. Turn left. The

Pose as Robin Hood

path drops downhill to another signposted crossroads. Turn left onto a public footpath, called Hangar Hill Drive, which is a surfaced track (5).

The woodland in this area once belonged to the Dukes of Portland who used it for recreational purposes, and one of the old rides can clearly be seen. Not content to just race through the woods, in 1724 the Duke of Portland bragged that 700 metres south of his home at Welbeck Abbey was a tree so huge that he could drive a coach and horses through it. Named the Greenwood Oak, this tree was so old and huge it was nicknamed 'The Methuselah of the Forest'. It is said to have been between 16-27 metres high, 700 to 1,400 years old, and capable of

sheltering 225 cattle – but time is a great exaggerator. Whatever the age, by 1664, the tree was showing signs of wear and tear worsened by the gales on 26th November, 1703, when many trees were uprooted and the Greendale Oak lost many branches.

To prove that he could indeed drive a coach and horses through this colossal specimen, the Duke made a wager with the Earl of Oxford, the wager was accepted and a massive archway over 3 metres in height was cut through the trunk. When the Duke of Portland drove a carriage pulled by two horses through the cavity he won his bet, but after this, understandably the Greendale Oak deteriorated rapidly and was soon propped up with sticks and chains holding the branches, until it was chopped down.

Statue of Robin and Little John in combat at the Visitor Centre

The vandalism is remembered in two pubs named The Greendale

Statue of Robin Hood carved in Sherwood Oak

Oak - one at Cuckney and one in Norfolk Street, Worksop, and the Countess of Oxford had a cabinet made with the cut wood, with engraved panels depicting the tree.

At a junction of tracks by Jerusalem Plantation (6) , turn right following the Robin Hood Way which becomes Green Drive. When the track bends sharply to the right to join Clipstone Drive, go downhill and continue straight ahead until reaching a less trodden footpath on your left by a yellow fire hydrant (7). Turn here and after ¼ mile you have reached the site of St Edwin's Chapel on your right (GR 596666).

King Edwin of Northumbria died in 632, in a battle with his pagan enemy King Penda of Mercia. Edwin's men gave him a secret burial in the forest clearing and a small chapel was built on the spot. It fell into ruin and would have disappeared forever if stones from the chapel had not been found when excavations were made in 1912. The Duke of Portland erected an iron cross and surrounded it with the stones - all that now marks the 7th century origins of Edwinstowe.

Keep to the track that runs alongside fields on your right until reaching a junction of tracks (8). Take the centre one – Crookdale Drive and follow this for ¾ mile until reaching a cross roads with Green Drive (9). Turn right and at the next junction, ignore the track on your right going south and the track on your left going north. At the Centre Tree where the tracks fork, take the right track (10) and follow this east for one mile. At a T junction (11) turn right and after 500 metres you will be back at the Sherwood Forest Art and Craft Centre Car Park which is the start/end of this walk.

Walk 5:
Wellow and The Maypole

Wellow is a small village that still practices its strong countryside traditions. It is one of only three villages in the country to have a permanent 60ft maypole on the village Green. There's the remains of a ducking stool near the dam, the medieval open field system is in place, and there's evidence of a former Norman Castle. Wellow was also featured in the children's book *The Secret World of Polly Flint* written by Helen Cresswell, which later became a TV series.

Distance	5 miles (8.10km)
Starting point	Wellow Dam
How to get there	Wellow is 1½ miles south/south-east of Ollerton along the A616 Wellow Road. Just before entering the village where roads go off to left and right and the main road veers right, take the minor road ahead signed to Wellow Dam
Parking	Wellow Dam Car Park
Map	Ordnance Survey OS Explorer 270
Map reference	GR 668664

The Robin Hood connection
All the tales of Robin Hood and his outlaw gang state that they were committed to a life of concealment in the forest – permanent exile in the greenwood, but when the damp fogs of Autumn hung over the bare woods, and the harsh frosts and snows of winter lasted for months, would they not be tempted to seek other more comfortable habitats? If it was safe to do so, many of the men might have returned to their old homes, but it is also possible that the outlaws could count

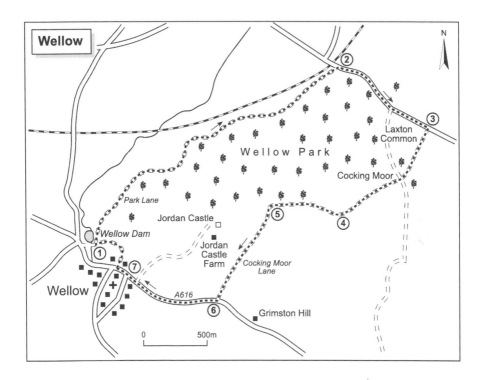

on the local Saxon lords for food and shelter in times of need. Amongst that number would undoubtedly have been Richard Foliot and his son Jordan, who in the 13th century occupied Jordan Castle at Wellow. This was a fortified castle, two days ride from Nottingham, concealed in dense woodland in the heart of Sherwood Forest, so what better place for our hero to reside.

Sadly the castle which stood at the north east of the village was allowed to fall into ruin. Now only the earthworks of Jordan Castle can be seen, but it's still quite atmospheric and a strong link with Robin and his outlaw gang.

The Walk

The walk starts from Wellow Dam (1), which was originally formed to provide water for the dyke encircling the village. The spring that fed it is now piped underground.

Local women were ducked in Wellow Dam as a form of punishment

The dam was originally much larger, and at least 12 metres closer to the village, encroaching upon what is now the car park. If you go to the centre of the car park, you'll see an ancient, almost concealed stone that was located at the edge of the larger dam. This is the remains of the village ducking stool preserved as a punishment for women accused of being a scold, a gossip or a wanton, and was used to dissuade old souls from the so-called practice of witchcraft. Over the stone would be placed a log with an iron stool on one end. The victim was strapped to the stool and with two men operating the counter-balanced end, the log was then swung out over the water and the victim immersed. The punishment was village entertainment. It attracted quite a crowd, and was fun for everyone but the poor unfortunate victim.

From the car park next to Wellow Dam take the track down the right hand side of the dam. This clear path then leads into and follows the edge of Wellow Park for 1½ miles along Park Lane. When reaching a T-junction with Cocking Hill (2), turn right and walk uphill for ½ mile, ignoring the first bridleway at the end of the woodland on your right. After 200 metres (3) take the next track on your right that goes through Laxton Common, across a field with a ditch on your right. The path leads through woodlands and soon begins to follow the edge of the wood. Eventually the path bends to the right around a field corner (4).

Go through a gate and turn left onto a track which heads gently downhill and bends to the left. When the track bends to the right to Jordan Castle Farm, continue ahead (5).

Jordan Castle Farm stands next to the mound on which Jordan Castle stood, although every last vestige appears to have been removed. The moat can be traced, and the three large parallel trenches running up and down the mound on the north-east and south-west sides are all that remain of the roadways that led to the castle.

Jordan Castle ceased to be occupied around the year 1425, although it served as a farm house for a further 100 years. It's status was further reduced when it became an animal shelter, and as it fell into a state of dilapidation it was quarried for its stone, which built many local houses.

Go through a gate onto Cocking Moor Lane that leads to the A616 near the site of the pinfold (6), a stone enclosure for holding stray livestock. Turn right and follow the road into Wellow (7).

Approaching the village green look for the 16th century Rock House, probably the oldest house in the village, over on your right next to the Old Village School. It is built on bedrock and has an overhanging upper storey facing the road. A little further along is The Durham Ox, one of the two Wellow public houses, and the site of a former coaching inn, catering for passengers as they travelled along the Great Way of Blyth.

Opposite is the village green and its 60ft maypole. The present maypole is made of steel and was erected in 1976; earlier versions were made of timber from Sherwood Forest. Happily old traditions like Maypole dancing, although now relatively low key, still take place in some villages to celebrate May Day, the first day of Celtic summer. This prime festival of pastoral England is rooted in pagan fertility rites when country folks rambled through the green woods on May Eve, returning home as the sun rose, laden with branches of may blossom to deck their homes and welcome summer. Whole villages joyfully 'brought in May' – a phrase embracing both the month and the sweet-smelling white hawthorn blossom. The day was spent in merrymaking with maypole dancing and rural sports, and many people believe that the Robin Hood legend stems from the May Day character 'Jack in the Green'. This was a man who danced inside a wood or basketwork frame that covered him from head to ankles until the visual effect was of a conical bush on feet. He's often confused with the so called 'Green Man' the foliated head to be found on many churches.

The village green has been eroded over the centuries by footpaths, buildings and the construction of Eakring Road but its original shape was a perfect isosceles triangle, the precise shape of the iron arrow heads made in the 12th and 13th centuries. Even more remarkable is the orientation. This symbolic arrow head is pointing directly at Nottingham Castle.

The second pub is the Red Lion on the eastern edge of the green, and next to it is the church of St Swithins built around 1189, during the reign of Richard I, with 19th century repairs and alterations. Of particular interest is the stained glass window depicting dancing round the village maypole.

Return to the main A616 and turn left, passing Wellow Hall to the right.

As we cross the Gorge Dyke at the entrance to the village, look for the remains of the drawbridge foundations on the left at the bottom of the dyke which once surrounded the village. The size of these stones would indicate that this was a drawbridge of considerable size at the point nearest to the King's Great Highway. The dyke is still traceable all around the perimeter of the village and is now designated an ancient monument.

Cross Dam Green to return to the car park which is the start/end of this walk.

Wellow Village Green with its 60ft maypole

Walk 6:
Clumber Park

The Dukeries, a collection of former ducal estates, lie in the northern part of Sherwood Forest, and the most popular and accessible is Clumber Park, now owned by the National Trust. Although the house has gone, the chapel, lake and parkland remain, with nearly 4000 acres of grassland, woodland and heath, a paradise for walkers and cyclists.

Clumber Park was once the country seat of the Dukes of Newcastle. Originally part of the great Sherwood Forest, in 1697 the first Duke of Newcastle enclosed 3,800 acres for use as a deer park. The second Duke transformed it into a landscaped park with the superb serpentine lake to complement Clumber House, their grand mansion, built in 1770. Rising costs and taxations caused the great house to be abandoned in the 1930s, and in 1938 it was demolished. All that now remains is the stable block and the Duke's study used by the National Trust as a shop, information centre and restaurant.

It was the second Duke who is credited with developing the Clumber Spaniel, the heavyweight of the spaniel world, the progenitors of

Distance	3½ miles (5.6km)
Starting point	The National Trust shop, information centre and restaurant. There is a vehicle entry charge
How to get there	Take the A1, then the A614 just south of Worksop
Parking	Car parks in the park
Maps	Ordnance Survey OS Explorer 270
Map reference	GR 621738 (Clumber Bridge)

which are the Alpine Spaniel, the St Bernard and the Basset Hound. This aristocratic gun dog is a veritable bulldozer of a dog amongst other sylph-like gun dogs. Even in its heyday as a working dog, the Clumber Spaniel was not built for speed, but neither was the mature sportsman who, like the Duke himself, were slowed down by years of good living.

Robin Hood connection
In Robin Hood's day, this area would have been rough heath and forest with a narrow river called The Poulter running through. It was then in the very heart of Sherwood forest, a royal hunting forest.

The Walk

With your back to the buildings (1), take the tarmac path that passes to the left of the toilet block, and at a T-junction turn left. Where the track bends right, keep ahead and make you way down to the lake (2), one of the most attractive parts of Clumber Park.

Clumber Bridge

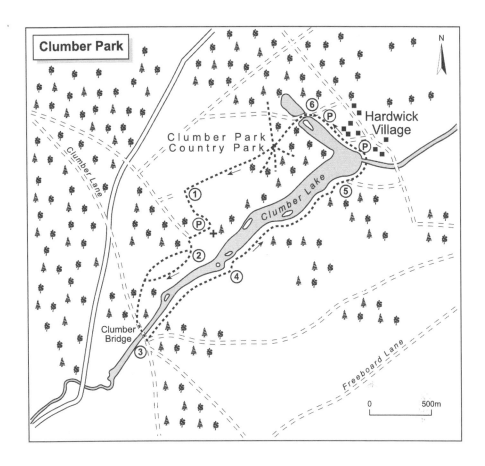

The great lake was created when the River Poulter was dammed to compliment the new landscaping scheme laid out by the Dukes of Newcastle. Beginning in 1772, the lake was built over a period of 15 years and cost £6,612. It extends over 32 hectares, and from the bridge in the west to the dam in the east the distance is 1.5 miles. Until the 1930s a small chain ferry was used to cross it. There was a cable on both banks and the remains of the winches can still be seen. Boats were once a feature here and in the early 1800s the Duke of Newcastle employed a sailor on the lake. There was a resident model frigate called The Lincoln, although it caught fire and sank to the bottom during World War II. Some of the wood is at times visible.

Turn right along the lakeside path through trees to a road just to the right of the elegant 18th century bridge spanning the narrowest point between the River Poulter and the lake (3).

Clumber Bridge was built by Stephen Wright in 1770, at the same time as Clumber House (demolished in 1938). The classical bridge is in a pale ashlar stone, has three almost semi-circular arches and a balustraded parapet.

Turn left over the bridge, pausing to admire the fine view of the lake fringed by trees.

Clumber can boast of having 120 different varieties of trees. In the background is the spire of the chapel which is visible for much of the way.

On the other side of the bridge, turn left along a tarmac track, pass through a car park and continue along a track beside the lake (4).

As you proceed through areas of woodland, the views are particularly impressive; to the right across grassland and to the left across the lake to the chapel and remains of the house.

Eventually bear left around the end of the lake (5), cross a footbridge and keep ahead, still beside the water.

To the right is the 19th century estate village of Hardwick, a name that means 'sheep farm', a clue to the hilly and wooded pastureland on which Hardwick was built.

John Fletcher, writer, local historian and expert on the Dukeries, told me a most interesting story about a man who approached him with the following story. The man, who visits Clumber Park regularly for recreational purposes, one day noticed a cottage deep in the woods. He couldn't remember seeing it before, but it had all the signs of habitation including children playing in the garden, so at the time he didn't think anything was amiss. Walking in the same area some time later, he couldn't find the cottage and this perplexed him so much that he returned time and time again to make a more thorough search. Having no success, he asked John's advice and John was able to tell him that there was no cottage and according to his early maps, there never had been any form of habitation in that area. So had this man experienced a time slip – a past scenario in a present day setting? Is it possible that in Robin Hood's day there might have been several cottages on this site, or even a small Saxon village?

There are numerous deserted medieval villages. The desertion and disappearance of this former village may have followed a similar pattern to many which were deemed unprofitable and therefore expendable to the feudal manorial landlords of the Middle Ages.

An archaeological dig might one day settle the matter but the huts in which the villagers lived would have had wattle and daub walls with heather-thatched roofs. Once the people had moved out, the harsh elements would have reclaimed these natural building materials until they had totally vanished from the landscape. Sadly time slips can't be used as indisputable evidence that a small medieaval community was here in Robin Hood's day, but its an interesting concept.

Follow the track through woodland

On reaching a tarmac drive (6), bear left to cross a bridge over an arm of the lake, then bear left again on to a track. Follow it through thick woodland, pass beside a barrier, cross a track and keep ahead, passing another barrier.

The track later becomes a tarmac drive and after passing a group of buildings on the left, turn left down another tarmac drive beside the car park. Where the drive heads right, keep ahead through iron gates and bear right along a path that passes in front of the chapel. From here, the path leads back to the information centre which is the

Walk 7:
Blyth

Blyth is a large, handsome village with a dignified air and a long history. It has yielded Bronze Age relics, skeletons that attest the presence of early man, and Roman coins. The former Benedictine Priory of St Mary, founded here in 1088, sat at the north end of the village, now marked by a noble Norman church, that claims to be one of the architectural glories of the county.

Blyth attained distinction during the time of the Norman Conquest, when it was included among the 174 manors in Nottinghamshire granted by William the Conqueror to one of his favourite Norman knights, Roger de Busli. The village occupied elevated ground surrounded by marshy, infertile land but what gave it prominence was the fact that it lay on the King's Great Highway, the ancient track

Distance	3½ miles (5.65km)
Starting point	The village green in the centre of Blyth
How to get there	Blyth is situated only just off the A1, N.NE of Worksop. From Doncaster in the north, Blyth is immediately off junction 34 of the A1(M) presently the last junction on the motorway south of the M18 intersection. From Nottingham in the south, take the A614 which joins the A1 a few miles after Ollerton
Parking	Roadside parking in Blyth centre
Map	Ordnance Survey OS Explorer 279
Map reference	SK 625872

between London and York, and at the important route centre of Stone Street or the Great Way of Blyth as it was often called. These two important highways that intersected the village were believed to date from Roman times and no doubt would have been tracks way before then.

Until recently, Blyth was a major staging post on the Great North Road, (later the A1) as its unusually wide main street and former coaching inns testify. Now it is bypassed by the main routes, leaving it as a quiet, attractive backwater with cottages grouped around a triangular green.

The Robin Hood connection
Blyth is mentioned in the earliest written story, *The Lytell Geste of Robin Hood*, which begins with Robin suggesting that Little John and Will Scathelocke find a paying guest to dine with them. When they encounter an impoverished knight and offer the invitation, the knight replies; 'My purpose was to have dined today at Blyth or Doncaster.' Instead he dines in the greenwood with Robin and his men, tells them his sad tale and gains their help and friendship. His name was Sir Richard of Lee.

In the same ballad, monks travelling from York to London are stopped in a similar way and invited to dine, a privilege for which they have to pay dearly. As the monk said; 'Me rue I came so near, for better cheap I might have dined in Blyth or Doncaster'.

In the days of Robin Hood, most monastic establishments like the Benedictine Priory of St Mary acted rather like our modern motorway service centres and hotel chains, where travellers were encouraged to break their journeys. Eventually as more and more pilgrims began travelling along the roads, the monasteries couldn't cope and inns were opened to provide food and overnight shelter. The Angel Inn in Blyth claims to be the oldest in the shire. It even has a bill dating from 1274 for the night's entertainment of the Bishop of Durham and his retinue. The total amount was 89s.7½d (almost £4.50) of which 33s.5d (£1.67½p) was for wine.

Blyth in those days lay on the northern fringe of Sherwood Forest and was one of the largest towns in the shire. It was also one of only five places in England licensed for tournaments. Could that be the reason the priory was set up here? It has been suggested that the monastic brethren, with their knowledge of curative herbs, potions and elementary surgery, ministered to those knights wounded in the jousts and performed the last rights to those who died there.

The foundation of the priory, the tournaments, its market and fair, meant that Blyth flourished under the Plantagenets. Agriculture and wool were its industries. There was considerable traffic on the road and travellers so often sought shelter at the priory that it obtained compensating relief from taxation. Kings and Archbishops were constant visitors, and it is highly likely that this prosperous little town would have been very familiar to Robin Hood and his men. It would have afforded them very rich pickings.

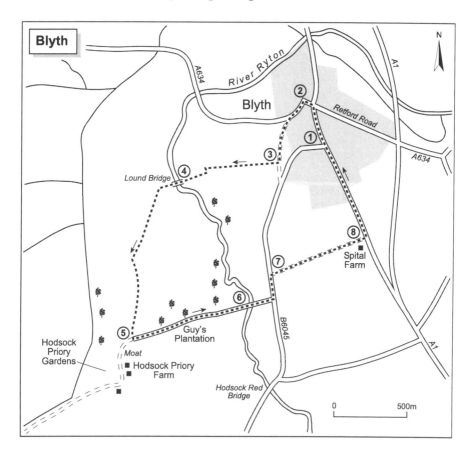

The Walk

Our walk begins at the village green (1) where there is plenty of roadside parking. Walk towards the priory and turn left at a T-junction in front of it.

A few ruins and the 11th century nave, which has been incorporated into the Norman church, are all that is left of Blyth priory, said to be the earliest monastic building in Nottinghamshire. The monastery lay on the north side, separated from the church by the cloisters and garth or open area, and Blyth Hall covers the site of some of the domestic buildings.

Follow the road around a sharp bend (2) and where it curves right, turn left along a tree lined track passing between gate-posts.

Climb a stile, continue ahead and take the first turning on the right (3) to walk along a straight track between fields. Later, keep by a hedge on the right and gently descend into the shallow valley of the River Ryton (4). All around are wide and extensive views. Climb a stile in the bottom corner of the field, bear left to climb another, continue across the left edge of a field and cross a footbridge over the river. Follow the path ahead through a small wooded area and continue beside a ditch on the left.

Look out for a wayward marker which directs you to turn left to cross the ditch. Bear right, then follow a path diagonally across a field. On the far side turn left along a track, and at a yellow marker turn right to continue along the left edge of a field, by a hedge on the left. Turn left over a waymarked stile and walk across the field ahead, veering slightly to the right in the direction of a large house. Go through a gate then follow a track across a field and go through another gate on a tarmac drive (5).

Bronze Age, Roman and Saxon farmers shaped the early landscape of Hodsock, and evidence of their food and household rubbish is still being found. A house at Hodsock was recorded in the 1086 Domesday Book, and those early owners were sufficiently powerful to entertain at least three kings – Henry II, John and Edward I. In the fifteenth century the estate passed to the Clifton family who owned it for fourteen generations and, in 1541 they entertained another king, Henry VIII. In 1765, the Hodsock estate was sold for the first and only time to the Mellish family, who owned the neighbouring estate of Blyth. Joseph Mellish was disinherited for extravagance and his brother lost the Blyth estate through gambling debts, but the estate passed to their sister Mrs Ann Chambers. Both Mrs Chambers and Mrs Margaret Mellish who inherited from Mrs Chambers, are responsible for the building we see today, which sadly is not open to the public. They also gave it the name Priory despite there being no evidence of a monastic nature.

Hodsock Priory Gardens are to the right, but turn left along the drive for just over ½ mile (800m) skirting Guy's Plantation, and re-crossing the River Ryton (6) to reach the road. Cross over and turn left towards Briber Hill, and at a public footpath sign turn right (7), continuing along the straight tarmac drive to Spital Farm.

Hodsock Priory dates back to the 11th century, but there's evidence of even earlier occupation

The name 'spital' in Spital Fields and Spital Farm is short for hospital. Blyth had two leper hospitals. The hospital of St John was founded in 1216 by William de Cressy, Lord of Hodsock, and in 1446 was rebuilt as a lodging house for 'strangers and women in labour'. The second, the hospital of St Edmunds, was built near the north gate of the priory in 1228 and was entirely dependent upon casual alms, its agents being officially licensed to beg for its maintenance. It was used as a school from 1695.

Head gently uphill. The tower of Blyth Priory Church can be seen to the left and continue between farm buildings to a road (8). Turn left and walk downhill to arrive at the village green in the centre of Blyth which is the start/end of this walk.

Walk 8: Ravenshead – Newstead Park – Papplewick

Distance	6¼ miles (10.10km)
Starting point	Ravenshead
How to get there	Ravenshead sits along the eastern side of the A60 between Mansfield and Nottingham. If approaching from the north, go through the traffic lights with the B6020 and after ¾ mile, almost opposite the entrance to Newstead Abbey, turn left into the car park of The Hut
Parking	The car park of The Hut, with the landlord's permission
Map	Ordnance Survey OS Explorer 270
Map reference	GR 557544

The Robin Hood connection

Newstead Abbey was never actually an Abbey; it was the Augustinian priory of St Mary, begun in 1163, and it's possible that the monastic cell at Fountain Dale, home of Friar Tuck was attached to this monastery. As Robin was definitely not on friendly terms with members of the monastic establishment, he most certainly would not have been a frequent visitor here, yet the King's Great Highway that passed by would have been regularly targeted for its rich pickings. Here he could select wealthy monks and bishops travelling in either direction along the King's Great Highway, a short length of which still runs past Papplewick Hall Gates to Newstead.

This made Papplewick one of Robin's favourite locations, near enough to Nottingham to travel here frequently, yet far enough away to avoid the constant harassment of the Sheriff's men. If there were any problems, here at Papplewick, Robin had a contingency plan. He had horses stabled, ready to leave the area in a hurry. A hidden cave is still known today as Robin Hood's Stables, yet without guidance, it's as well hidden as it was in Robin's day. It could have been a medieval hermitage because it's a spacious, dry dwelling 16ft high, dug out of the soft sandstone with a scooped out shelf probably used for the horse's manger or a hermit's bed. The cave is now on private property so permission to view, and instructions to find, must be obtained by writing to The Hermitage at Papplewick.

Robin Hood's stables, a well hidden cave in private woodland

St James' Church, Papplewick is often referred to as The Forester's Church, because during the middle ages the wardens of Sherwood Forest were based at Papplewick

The Walk

From the car park, look across the road to the main entrance of Newstead Abbey Park, where you will see the Pilgrim tree said to date back to medieval times. By tradition, pilgrims met under this tree before passing on to the priory.

Leave the car park (1) at the narrow, northern end and turn right along the A60 taking the footpath to the left of The Hollies - signed for St Peter's church. At the junction with Sheepwalk Lane (2) turn left and continue for ½ mile, passing the modern church as you proceed. At the T-junction with the B6020, Main Road to Blidworth, bear left uphill to reach the traffic lights on the A60 after 400 yards. Cross the A60

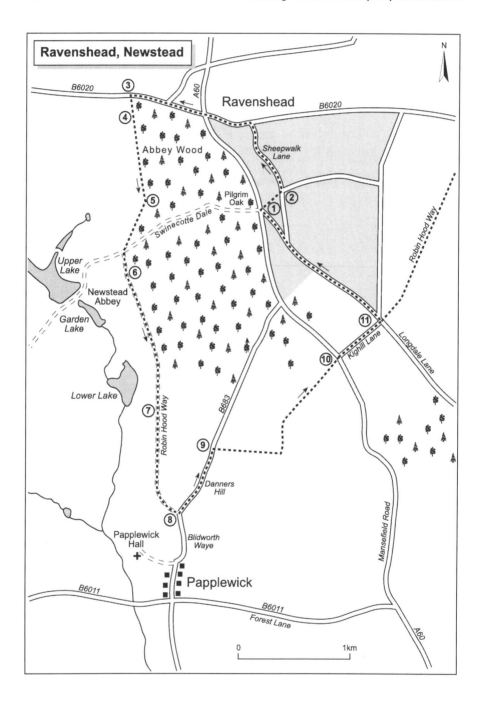

carefully and walk along Kirby Road. After ½ mile, immediately after the last house on the left, No 51, turn left (3) at a stile to follow the Robin Hood Way. Take a left turn then a right onto the Woodland Trust Property.

The path runs parallel to a stone wall on the left just a few yards away, then between the wall on the left and various red-brick properties – a former hospital – on the right (4). Keep forward to reach an open field on your right. Stay on the left side of this. The path then dips into a hollow at the end of the field.

Ignore the path to the right (5), and climb the steps to enter the woodland. This is full of oak trees, beech and silver birches. The path forks at the point where ahead of you at the bottom of a slope, you'll see a tarmac lane – Swinecotte Dale. Keep forward to the lane, ignoring the right fork which leads to Newstead Abbey, and the Upper Lake, and rise up the path beyond. You subsequently join a single track tarmac lane (6) where you bear left. A little way after this, there is a seat on the right and a view of the Abbey.

After the dissolution of the monasteries, the ruined Augustinian priory was purchased by Sir John Byron of Colwick, for £810, and he converted the monastic buildings into an Elizabethan country mansion. The estate passed through five successive Sir John Byrons, and with each generation, the family fortunes dwindled until when the 5th Sir John Byron died, in 1798, the title and wreckage of the estate passed to his ten year old great nephew, George Gordon Byron, the famous poet.

Byron sold Newstead Abbey for £100,000 to Thomas Wildman, an old school friend who spent a fortune on 'doing it up'. On his death in 1860 the property was purchased by WF Webb, who's descendants owned the Abbey until 1931 when Sir Julien Cahn bought it and gave it to the City of Nottingham as a home for the collections of Byron memorabilia that remains there.

Unfortunately all that now remains of the Abbey is the west front, the wall of the church that backs onto the west cloister, and the shell of the wings around the rest of the cloisters. The present chapel was the monks' chapter house and the odd room next door, in medieval times, the slype or passageway.

An early drawing of Newstead Abbey

Our walk continues along Hall Lane which is part of the Robin Hood Way along the edge of Abbey Wood.

This is also part of the medieval King's Great Highway linking Newstead with Papplewick. This was the motorway of its day along which the clergy and merchants transporting money and goods, so it offered rich pickings for the outlaws.

The lane loses height and is then a steady straight walk (7) for a while before reaching a former lodge. Keep to the right of the driveway to pass through an old metal kissing gate, then continue ahead on what becomes a gravel drive for 1¼ miles until reaching the B683, Blidworth Waye, north of Papplewick (8). You may be tempted to walk into Papplewick in which case, turn right.

Over on your right is Papplewick Hall built, in 1787, by Sir Frances Montagu, Lord of the Treasury, and designed by the Adam brothers.

St James' Church, Papplewick is often referred to as The Forester's Church because during the middle ages the wardens of Sherwood Forest were based at Papplewick. In the floor are old gravestones of past foresters, decorated with carvings of bows, arrows and the forester's hunting horn. The wardens of Sherwood would have been sworn enemies of the outlaws, so it's unlikely that Robin and his men worshipped at Papplewick, although some tales say Allan a Dale was married here, a distinction shared with Steetley.

To continue our walk, turn left along Blidworth Waye, crossing to the far side of the road where there is a narrow path beyond the ditch. Some 60 yards later, follow the Robin Hood Way as it enters the wood. This proceeds with the road to your left and is a much pleasanter and safer option than the road. Leave the wood and use the right hand verge beside the road for 70-80 yards. You then have the chance to walk through another narrow roadside wood until again you have to come out beside the road. Continue on the verge beyond for 130 yards or so.

On reaching the entrance to Newstead Grange on the left, turn right (9) and walk away from the road for 500 yards beside a hedge on your right. In the bottom corner of the field turn left for 250 yards then bear right into the plantation. Keep on the same line to enter what looks like heathland. Continue through this to reach a track at the top of the bank ahead of you. Turn left here before, 50 yards later, turning right to cross the track, and walk up the right side of the wood ahead. Stay beside the fence on your right as it bears left then right to walk to the main road, the A60 ahead (10).

Cross the road carefully and walk along Kighill Lane for 500 yards. Turn left into Longdale Lane and, for ¾ mile, ignore all roads off to the right and subsequently some to the left. This brings you back to The Hut which is the start/end of this walk.

Walk 9: Fountain Dale and Friar Tuck's Trail

This is a stunning woodland walk in the heart of outlaw country, passing the site at Fountain Dale where Robin Hood first met Friar Tuck, then continuing on to Blidworth, the home village of Maid Marion. There's a number of interesting things to discover on the way, including a Druid Stone, a folly built from the stone of an earlier church and a number of unusual monuments, including one to the outlaw Will Scarlet.

Distance	6 miles (9.70km)
Starting point	Harlow Wood
How to get there	Take the A60 Mansfield – Nottingham road. One mile north of the junction of the B6020 turn into the Greenwood Craft and Garden Centre, Portland College for the Disabled
Parking	Ample free parking is available in the car park of the centre
Map	Ordnance Survey OS Explorer 270
Map reference	GR 552568

The Robin Hood connection
There always appears to be conflict when Robin meets the men who will later be his followers, and his first encounter with Friar Tuck is no exception. The two men dispute the right of way across the stream, and when neither will concede, each in turn carries the other across on his back until Robin is tossed into the water. Robin threatens to call his men and Friar Tuck threatens to call his pack of hounds, but in the

end all is forgiven and Friar Tuck becomes one of the outlaw band.

Their meeting at Fountain Dale is not improbable as there was an ancient route through the forest passing close to where, according to the ballad *Robin Hood and the Curtal Friar*, Friar Tuck had a hermitage. Friar Tuck baptising his converts at this spot where a chalybeate spring fed a shallow bath of water, and this is now known as Friar Tuck's well. The last ruinous stones from the old hermitage were apparently only removed as late as 1875.

When Robin Hood and the Friar dispute the right of way, the Friar carries Robin across the stream (H Pyle)

We walk on to Blidworth, reputedly the home village of Maid Marion, and the last resting place of Will Scarlet marked by a rather unusual monument in the graveyard.

The Walk

Leave the Craft Centre (1) , cross the access road and walk south away from the café and car park, taking the track opposite by the buildings. Shortly you will locate marker posts with white tops. These mark the route to follow on the Friar Tuck trail.

Continue along the track, parallel to the A60 road seen through the plantation on your right until reaching a 90 degree left hand bend (2). At this point the Robin Hood Way comes in from the right. If you want a slight detour, take the Robin Hood Way right, which takes you back to the A60, turn left and just down on your left is the Sheppard Stone.

Back in 1817, a local girl from Papplewick named Elizabeth (Bessie) Sheppard was murdered in these woods and a stone was erected by the side of the A60 to mark the spot. When the road was widened, the stone

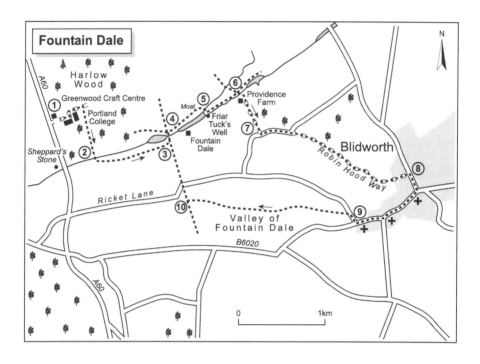

was moved to its new position and the worn engraving was replaced, leaving us a sad reminder of her murder in Harlow Wood.

From point (2), continue to follow the marked path across partly wooded heath land for 1km until reaching a crossing of tracks with telegraph wires above. Straight ahead is the first of the Fountain Dale Lakes and Friar Tuck's shelter (3). Continue for 200 metres to a crossing of tracks (4) and follow the footpath straight ahead to Fountain Dale, first passing The Moat.

This excavation, about 200 yards long is H shaped. The south trench of The Moat is where the stream ran before the lake was excavated but, because the course of the stream was altered, the lake gets full of water while The Moat now has a low level of stagnant water. Many years ago, a simple wooden footbridge spanned The Moat and a notice board proclaimed that this was the spot where Robin Hood and Friar Tuck disputed the right of way.

About 100 yards further along is Friar Tuck's Well.

Prior to the sale of the Fountain Dale estate, in 1952, Friar Tuck's well had been surrounded by ornamental railings and covered by thick stone slabs, then an old beech tree blew down in a gale, destroying the railings and the slabs disappeared. All that can now be seen are the stones lining the cavity of the well. The spring periodically dries up, as do all the springs from this point westward, to the stream's source near the Nottingham/Mansfield Road. According to legend, the valley stays dry for 7 years, due to Friar Tuck imposing a curse because of a grievance. It is now dry, overgrown and barely discernable, although at times there is a low level of stagnant water.

Sir Walter Scott stayed at Fountain Dale House in 1822 while he penned part of Ivanhoe. He called the area Copmanhurst. His hero, Ivanhoe, was another social rebel and freedom fighter, an almost carbon-copy version of Robin Hood, who Sir Walter Scott introduced as a character in Ivanhoe, as Robin of Loxley.

Leave Friar Tuck's Well and continue until reaching a junction of paths by Providence Farm (6). Turn right go through a gate and, keeping right of the farm, the path joins the farm's access road, which brings you to a lane which is part of the Robin Hood Way (7). Turn left and follow this track for just over a mile. This is New Lane and forms a T-junction with the B6020 Mansfield Road at Blidworth (8). Turn right and follow the main road through Blidworth.

Blidworth (pronounced locally Blidduth) has always been regarded as the home village of Lady Marion. In those days, the houses and cottages clustered round the main street just below the church, and she reputedly lived in a house on the site next to the present Ashfield Cottage, near The Black Bull Inn. There are still the extensive, cavernous cellars which date back hundreds of years and some, disturbed in recent years, can be seen near the side of the road.

An old custom that still survives in Blidworth is the rocking ceremony. This involves taking the male child baptised nearest to the first Sunday in February and rocking him in a cradle lined with flowers. The child is then paraded round the streets in a carnival atmosphere. The custom lapsed but was reintroduced in 1922.

Continue along the Main Street until reaching The Bird in Hand on your left.

With its spectacular views south across the valley, this would have been a likely spot for Robin and his outlaw gang to loiter over a drink at the old ale house where they would pick up information and gain plenty of warning of passing travellers.

A few yards further is Blidworth church, dedicated to St Mary of the Purification. This church was built in the 15th century to replace an earlier building, part of which is still in the churchyard.

When the church was to be rebuilt in 1839, Mrs Need of Fountain Dale salvaged parts of the medieval church that would otherwise have been thrown away as rubble. She had window surrounds, coffin slabs and a doorway taken to Fountain Dale. When Newstead Colliery Company bought Fountain Dale at the beginning of the 20th century, the

The ruins of an earlier church at Blidworth

incumbent vicar, Revd RH Whitworth ensured that all the rescued pieces of the old medieval church were moved back to the church yard. G Wells of Caunton erected them, following no particular plan, and now they form an attractive folly.

Another point of interest in the churchyard is the cross 20 metres away, facing the church's south porch. According to the story, this is Tom Leake's cross. Tom Leake was a forest ranger besotted by the daughter of the landlady of The Archer, a pub of low repute. She apparently also had other admirers including Captain Salmon of Salterford Hall, and in 1597 the jealous captain killed 60 year old Leake in a duel. A cross was erected where Leake fell, but by 1751 the cross had disintegrated and the remaining base was moved to the church. Along with the previously ment-ioned stones, this too was rescued by Mrs Need and taken to Fountain Dale from where it was returned to the churchyard.

And lastly, there is a belief that Will Scarlet is buried in Blidworth Churchyard. A rather bizarre pile of stones is pointed out as his monument. I was told that the top

The monument to Will Scarlet in Blidworth churchyard

stones came from the previous chancel and have been placed on top of an old baptismal font turned upside down. To view Will Scarlet's monument, pass through the gate immediately beyond the water-tap and it's straight ahead. Comparing its present position to a 1908 photograph taken with the church in the background, it seems to have been moved and shortened since, so don't assume that it marks Will's actual grave.

Leave the churchyard and turn left continuing out of Blidworth down the Main Street for ¼ mile until reaching Ricket Lane on your right (9). After a short distance, take the footpath to the left and follow the yellow markers for about 1,200 metres. Over in the field on your right is what is known as the Blidworth boulder (GR 579558), a stark isolated stone that stands 15ft high and is believed to be associated with the druids and their mysterious rituals

The huge stone in a field called Rock Close is a mass of clay and gravel, flat-topped, over 4 metres high and 8 metres in circumference. Towards the base is a large hole through which, in earlier centuries, children were passed in the belief that this would cure their whooping cough. It is mentioned in James Prior's novel 'Fortuna Chance'.

A number of other glacial deposits of this kind were left in this area of Blidworth during the Ice Age. In order not to hinder cultivation of the fields, the other smaller stones were blown up and the remains removed. This is the only survivor.

Continue through the valley of Fountain Dale for almost a mile, basically keeping straight ahead, guided by stiles until reaching a cross path (10). Turn right and shortly you will reach Ricket Lane. Cross the lane and continue straight ahead to Fountain Dale where you will join your previous route near the site of Friar Tuck's Hut (3). Retrace your steps back to Greenwood Craft Centre which is the start/end of this walk.

Walk 10: Rufford Abbey
Country Park – Edwinstowe

The first recorded owner of Rufford was a Saxon man called Ulf but, after the Norman conquest, William I gained the estate and gave it to his nephew Gilbert de Gant, who was also given the title the Earl of Lincoln. He founded Rufford Abbey, although its construction could have continued for a century, for a group of Cistercian monks, as a 'daughter ' house of Rievaulx Abbey in Yorkshire.

After the dissolution in 1536 the estate was granted to George Talbot the 4th Earl of Shrewsbury. The 6th Earl and his wife, Bess of Hardwick, converted it into a large country house. In 1626, the house passed from the Shrewsburys to the Saville family, who owned it for over three centuries (1626-1938).

Sir George Saville was the 7th baronet and did a great deal to improve the property. It was sold in 1938, and after a number of owners, in 1969, it passed into the hands of the Nottinghamshire Council. Today the remains of Rufford Abbey and all the park buildings are grade II listed ancient monuments in the care of English Heritage. It became a designated country park, and Rufford is now open daily until dusk and receives over half a million visitors each year. Admission is free,

Distance	5 Miles (8.10km)
Starting point	Rufford Abbey County Park
How to get there	Rufford County Park is 16 miles north of Nottingham, east of the old Rufford Road – A614, two miles south of Ollerton
Parking	Car park in Rufford Abbey
Map	Ordnance Survey OS Explorer 270
Map reference	SK 644648

although there is a parking charge at weekends, on bank holidays and
school holidays.

The Robin Hood connection

Rufford Abbey dates back to 1147, when it was built as a Cistercian
Abbey, yet the monks never seemed to be satisfied and grabbed all
the land around. Records show that they had twenty one granges and
farms and, in a fifteen year period, they felled 7,000 oaks and 1,000
saplings to clear forest land for farming. Their greed was unstoppable.
They took no account of the needs of the locals who relied on the
forest for their livelihood. The villages of Rufford, Cratley, Grimston,
Besthorpe, Winkerfield, Westhaw and Almton disappeared under their
onslaught. The people were moved out of their homes, often by force,

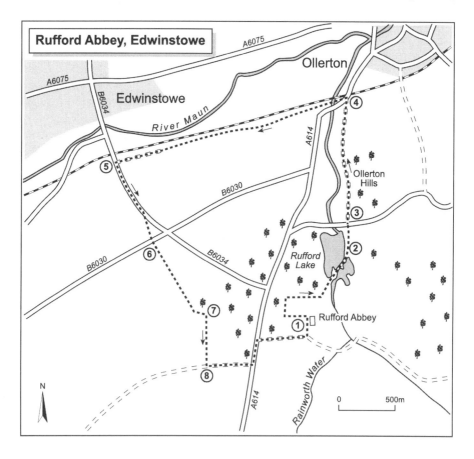

and this exploitation understandably made the monks very unpopular. This is just the kind of injustice that Robin Hood would have fought against.

With this kind of wholesale exploitation it's easy to see why the local peasants hated the monks almost as much as they hated the domineering Norman barons, so the tales of Robin and his men taking from the avaricious monks were always greeted with great enthusiasm. Robbing the king's collectors and wealthy monks was considered an honourable kind of thievery, if you could get away with it – and Robin seemed to be invincible.

The Walk

From the car park (1) take the path signposted to the Abbey. Turn left in front of the stable block and walk past the Abbey's remains on your right.

The educated Cistercian monks at the abbey copied books within the scriptorium, a special writing room, and used their creative skills to illuminate the manuscripts with gold leaf and beautiful embellished colours. The less educated monks reared sheep, and worked the fields and gardens. Together, the monks reorganised the roads so that any paths or highways that had previously run across their land were made to skirt round it and, as the monastic lands grew, they updated the maps recording the expanding boundaries of Rufford.

Continue ahead along a wide path lined with trees. This path turns at a right angle. At a T-junction turn left and then right at a crossroad of tracks. This clear path takes you across several bridges, then up the right hand side of the lake (2). The old mill complex can be seen at the end of the lake.

After passing the lake you reach a stile onto Rufford Lane (3). Climb it and cross the road to a path opposite, which takes you along a field edge. Initially the hedge is on your left, then on your right. You emerge onto the A614, Old Rufford Road, by a railway bridge (4). Cross over the road and climb a stile. This path leads to a footbridge which spans Rainworth Water and, shortly after the bridge, there is a stile on your left. Climb the stile and turn right. Continue in the same direction

along the edge of fields, with a fence and a railway line on your right, all the way into Edwinstowe.

On reaching the B6034 (5) turn left. Ten metres after passing Sandy Lane on your right, a signpost marks a path off to your right in between a fence and a hedge. Cross a road and pass the South Forest leisure centre on your left.

Cross over the B6030 (6) and take the path opposite, to join the Robin Hood Way, along a field edge with the hedge on your left. The path leads into woodland for 50 metres. At the end of the trees turn left and follow a field edge. This path bends to the right (7) and eventually leads to a T-junction (8). Turn left onto the wide track part surfaced, and continue until reaching the A624. Turn left, then after a short distance, right through the gates of Rufford Abbey Park to return to the car park which is the start/end of this walk.

Wooden carvings of Robin and his gang decorate this canopy at the entrance to Ma Hubbard's Inn

Walk 11: Creswell Crags and Robin Hood's Cave

Cresswell Crags is a limestone gorge tucked away within the gently undulating landscape on the Derbyshire/Nottinghamshire border. It's packed with fissures and caves that have yielded rich evidence of occupation by both man and beasts in prehistoric times. The site's Visitor Centre provides an interesting presentation of what life was like for the inhabitants of these caves.

Distance	1¾ miles (2.80km)
Starting point	Creswell Crags
How to get there	From the M1 junction 30, take the A616. After a short distance, cross the roundabout and head south/east along the A616 for almost 4 miles, passing through Clowne. Drive into Creswell, then take the B6042 road on your left. The caves and Creswell Crags Visitor Centre is signposted on your right off this road
Parking	Creswell Crags Visitor Centre Car Park
Map	Ordnance Survey OS Explorer 270
Map reference	GR 538743

The Robin Hood connection

Creswell Crags are mentioned in one of the Robin Hood Ballads, as the caves at Creswell were purportedly frequented by Robin Hood and his followers, and would have made a perfect hideout for the outlaw gang. It's therefore not surprising that here you will find Robin Hood Cave. There is also the Robin Hood Way just the other side of the A60 on the Derbyshire/Nottinghamshire border. In one of the Robin Hood

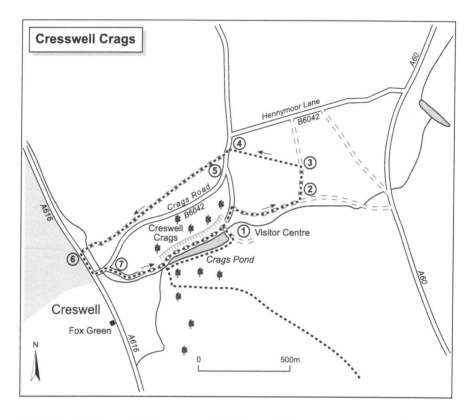

Ballads, Robin and his men trick Prince John into going to the crags to supposedly locate and capture the outlaw but, as usual, it's a hoax. Prince John and his men leave his palace at Clipstone undefended while they search the Crags, giving Robin and his men ample time to release the prisoners held in the dungeons at Prince John's Palace at Clipstone

The Walk

The walk begins at the Cresswell Crags Visitor Information Centre car park (1) and is walked in an anti-clockwise direction. Walk along the track away from the Creswell Crags Visitor Centre to a bar gate in approximately 100 yards. This path is part of the Robin Hood Way, the 88 mile route through Sherwood Forest from Nottingham Castle to Edwinstowe.

Turn left at the signed path (2) and follow a well defined farm track to Henneymoor Farm. Just before the first field boundary on your left (3), turn left and follow the grass track, keeping the hedge on your right to a small gate and bridlepath sign at the B6042, Henneymoor Lane, which leads to Whitwell.

From the B6042 road (4), turn left and, in 10 yards, turn right (5) leaving the road onto another bridleway with a metal bar gate. Keep on this well defined track for a little over ½ mile. It runs almost parallel to the B6042, and after passing Bank House Farm it meets the A616 Mansfield Road (6). Turn left, then left again into the B6042 at the traffic lights then right into Crags Road (7), which runs through the gorge around Crags Pond.

At the southern end of the pond, look out for Crags Cottage, which was once the Old Star Inn, and is the last building of a small settlement by a watermill which stood here.

In the 1700s the Duke of Portland engaged the painter George Stubbs to paint views of the Welbeck Estate. One, known as 'Two Gentlemen

Robin Hood's Cave at Creswell Crags

going Shooting' shows the mill and crags. The mill and thatched buildings were demolished in the 1860s, the mill pond was drained and the present lake was made by damming the stream to create an ornamental lake for recreational purposes.

The limestone crags that lie either side of the narrow gorge act as a boundary between Derbyshire and Nottinghamshire. There are five major caves that have been home to man since about 43,000 BC.

We need to be at the opposite end of the pond (8). If you'd like to do a full circuit to see the caves close to, it is necessary to duplicate one side, although the public are not allowed to explore the caves and metal grids prevent access.

Pin Hole Cave is named after a 19th century custom of every visitor dropping a pin into the rock pool at the entrance and making a wish. Robin Hood's Cave is the largest cave with four main chambers. Mother Grundy's Parlour was named after a witch who lived there last century; Boat House Cave is where the boat for the lake was kept, and Church Hole Cave extends 170 feet into the hillside and has yielded the finest artefacts from the area.

These caves could have been the earliest human dwelling in Britain, where evidence of Palaeolithic man has been discovered dating from before the first ice age, 50,000 years ago. Old Stone Age man shared his abode with the woolly rhinoceros, woolly mammoth, cave bear, hyena, wolf, wild horse, bison, reindeer, lynx, and cave lion.

A bone from Robin Hood's Cave was found engraved with a horse design and further excavations have uncovered more than eighty carvings depicting bison, deer, bear and birds. The discovery of this cave art is one of the most significant finds from early prehistory and much of the best carving is in Church Hole Cave. A 13,000 year old carving, discovered in July 2004, is said to be of a naked woman, so this would qualify it as the earliest nude in the history of British art.

Having reached the far side of the pond (8), follow the path down the steps with the stream on your right to the Visitor Centre and car park which is the start/end of this walk.

Walk 12: Steetley Chapel – where Allen a Dale wed his sweetheart

The village of Whitwell straddles the county borders of Derbyshire and Nottinghamshire, and on this walk we also pass the point marked by the Shireoak, where Derbyshire and Nottinghamshire meet Yorkshire – three counties in one walk. Whitwell is an interesting village with a rich history and some attractive buildings. As you enter the village, you will pass St Lawrence Church, a fine 12th century Norman church with 14th and 15th century additions, and just after the church is Old Hall Lane, which leads to Whitwell Hall, a 16th century manor house, owned by the Dukes of Rutland and later the Dukes of Portland. It's still a private residence and not open to the public. The Manor House on High Street is one of the oldest buildings in the village. The Old George Inn, now flats, was an eighteenth century coaching inn on the Chesterfield to Worksop turnpike road, and Lilac Cottage across from the George Inn was probably used as the inn's stables. Look out for The Old Blacksmith's Shop that has a wheelwright's stone built into the garden wall.

Distance	6 miles (9.70km)
Starting point	Whitwell
How to get there	From the M1 junction 30, take the A616. After a short distance, cross the roundabout and head east along the A619 for 1¾ miles. Turn right into the B6043 to Whitwell, following the High Street through until reaching the car park
Parking	Car park next to the Whitwell Health Centre
Map	Ordnance Survey OS Explorer 270 and 279
Map reference	GR 530767

Our walk takes us to Steetley chapel, now regarded as the finest example of Norman architecture in the country. It's a little gem, measuring just 52ft x 16ft, and is not marked on maps or road signs, but it has very strong connections with our outlaw band.

The Robin Hood connection
Steetley Chapel is the most perfectly preserved little Norman church, and undoubtedly one of the oldest and most attractive buildings in Sherwood forest. Built about 1140, by Gley de Briton as his private chapel, traditionally, Friar Tuck regularly took the outlaws here to pray. It's also said that Steetley Chapel had a false roof in which Robin and his men hid when necessary.

In the tale of Robin Hood and Allen a Dale, Robin intervenes to prevent Allen's sweetheart, Ellen, marrying an elderly Norman knight named Sir Stephen of Trent, a marriage arranged by her father, Edward of Deirwold, a stout Saxon franklin. Robin asks the distressed bride who she would prefer for a husband and when she names Allen a Dale, Sir Stephen is displaced and the marriage goes ahead with Ellen marrying Allen.

Although the church is not named, it is described as 'a certain little church that belonged to a private estate', and although we can never be 100% sure that this is the church, it's been accepted as such for hundreds of years.

The Walk

From the car park (1) turn right and right, again at the road junction. Heading uphill, take the first left onto Hangar Hill until meeting a T-junction onto Doles Lane. Turn right and, after 20 metres, turn left at a public footpath sign (2) and follow the clear winding track across fields to the A619 (3).

Cross over and join a rough track called Firbeck Lane, which eventually becomes a surfaced lane as it becomes Whitwell Road (4). On your left is Whitwell Wood, an ancient broadleaf woodland where evidence of early man has been found. As you reach a crossing of tracks (5), the infant Shireoak can be seen on your right. The original Shireoak marked the point where the counties of Derbyshire, Yorkshire and

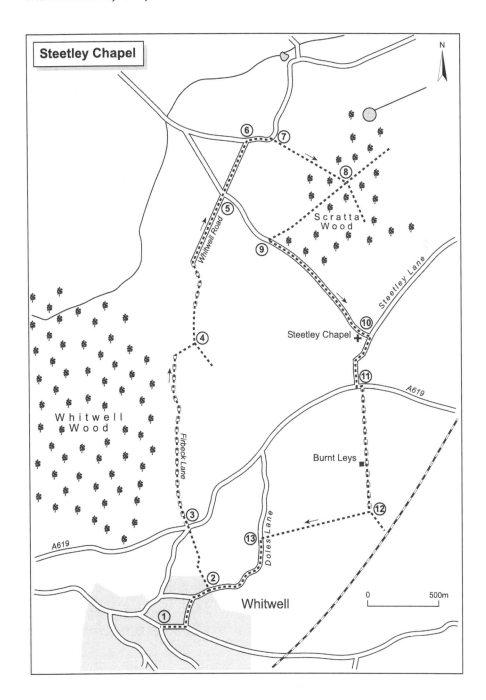

Nottinghamshire merged. At a crossroad of lanes, continue ahead then turn right at a T-junction into Netherthorpe Road (6).

Despite the fact that most people accept that Little John was buried in Hathersage, this area makes a rather startling claim. If you turn left and continue on this lane for a mile, you will reach Thorpe Salvin, where they state they have the last resting place of Little John in their graveyard.

Even more unexpected, there's a claim that Robin Hood (supposedly buried at Kirklees in Yorkshire) is allegedly buried in the farm next to Steetley churchyard, our next port of call.

From the T-junction (6) continue along Netherthorpe Road and, as the lane turns to the left, turn right at a signpost onto a track (7). Continue until meeting a crossroad of tracks (8) and turn right to follow the edge of Scatta Wood, which is on your right. This is another site where excavations have uncovered Iron Age and Stone Age settlements. On

The Norman chapel at Steetley where the outlaws hid and Allen a Dale was purportedly married

reaching Dumb Hall Lane (9) turn left. This becomes Scratta Lane. Continue along Scratta Lane until reaching Steetley Chapel on your right.

This small, secluded chapel is a Norman architectural gem built in 1120. The marvel is that this beautiful church has weathered so many storms. It stood deserted and derelict for over 200 years, was used for cockfighting, as a shed for lumber and as a sheepfold, yet was skilfully restored in 1882 and reconsecrated. It is now part of the parish of Whitwell and a service is held here every Sunday at 3.15 pm.

Although it seems quite out of proportion for such a small building, 56ft (16.8m) in length by 16ft (4.8m) wide, enter by the magnificent south doorway with its four round arches. The outer arch with zig-zag mouldings, rests on columns carved with signs of the zodiac, although these are now indecipherable as they've been damaged by exposure.

This tiny chapel has a massive chancel arch with a scene of Saint George slaying the dragon, and a second arch divides the chancel from the semi-circular apse at the end of the nave, a feature that was copied in many of the early Christian churches.

Leave the chapel and continue to the end of the lane (10), to turn right at the junction with Steetley Lane, and continue for 300 yards to the main A619 road (11). Cross with care and walk straight up the lane opposite to Burnt Leys Farm. The route heads past Burnt Leys Cottages and Burnt Leys Farm and becomes a rough track close to some large gates. After 150 metres, the track bends to the right (12). Continue until the track ends and it becomes a path across the middle of a field. This brings you to Doles Lane (13). Turn left and follow this through to Whitwell, down Hangar Hill to reach the car park which is the start/end of this walk.

Walk 13: The Grave of Little John and Robin Hood's Stoop

Places bearing the name Robin Hood and his loyal sidekick Little John are abundant in Derbyshire, especially around Hathersage, the alleged birth place and burial place of Little John. The hills and valleys of Derbyshire could have echoed to the sound of Robin Hood's hunting horn, as there are no shortage of links with the legendary medieval outlaw.

The graveyard of the church in the historical village of Hathersage – written Hereseige in 1086 – has to be the most visited in Derbyshire because it is the last resting place of Little John, Robin Hood's right hand man. Yet there is more to see than just the grave. This lovely walk takes you beside the River Derwent to Robin Hood's Stoop, and for refreshment there's The Little John Hotel, and The Scotsman's Pack where you'll find a chair alleged to have belonged to Little John.

A statue of Little John carved in Sherwood oak

The Robin Hood connection
From very early days, Hathersage was connected with the making of metal objects like pins and nails. According to tradition, John the Nailer was a giant of a man, spending his early working life making iron nails – and earning his surname – in his native village of Hathersage. His size and strength were put to good use, albeit on the losing side, when he fought under Simon de Montford at the Battle of Evesham in 1265, but when next heard of, he had become Little

Distance	4 miles (6.50km)
Starting point	Leadmill, one mile outside Hathersage
How to get there	Take the A6187 Sheffield to Castleton Road and in the centre of Hathersage turn into the B6001 to Grindleford. Follow this for one mile
Parking	Park in the car park of the Plough Inn just past Leadmill Bridge
Map	Ordnance Survey OS Explorer OL1 and OL24
Map reference	GR 234805

John, one of a marauding band of outlaws led by a man whose true identity was hidden behind the name of Robin Hood.

After Robin's death, legend has it that Little John returned to Hathersage to die in the cottage where he had been born, and after his death the ballad says :

Little John's cottage at Hathersage

His Bow was in the chancel hung, his last good bolt they drove
Down to the rocke, its measured length Westward fro' the grave
And root and bud this shaft put forth when Spring returned anon
It grew a tree and threw a shade where slept staunch Little John

His grave, which lies in the churchyard just opposite the main door, has huge yew trees at each

Little John's grave

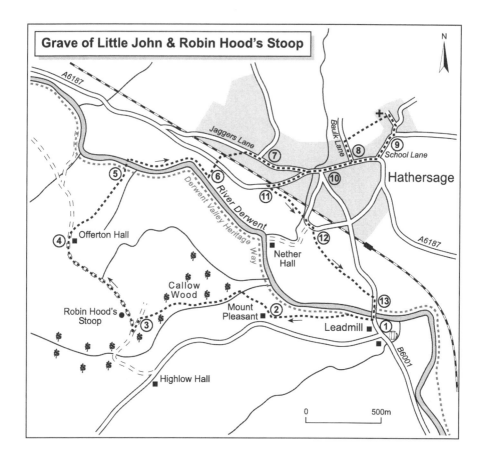

end, so could one of these have sprouted from Little John's 'last good bolt'? The churchyard contains some fine old Yew trees, the type that yielded the wood from which the medieval longbow was made.

The Walk

Leave the car park (1) and head back down the B6001 road as far as Leadmill Bridge, passing through the squeeze stile on the nearside just before the bridge. Follow the riverside path. After passing a derelict barn, bear left against a stile, leaving the river and ascending a steep bank. Cross a step-stile and turn right, following the edge of the field and continuing ahead to reach a farm lane at Mount Pleasant (2).

Turn right along the Broadhay farm track. Leave this after a while via a way marked footpath on the left. Pass through the gate and cross the field on the line of the overhead wires, with woods on either side. Continue through Callow Wood, then bear right at a junction of paths. You are now climbing steeply, but after emerging from the wood, turn left and ascend to Callow Farm (3). In the yard area, turn left to follow the drive until reaching a fork in the lane. Turn right and after a few yards Robin Hood's stoop (GR 217807) is over on your left on the edge of Offerton Moor.

A stoop is a three or four sided stone used as a guide post and positioned at the intersection of old pack horse routes. Stoops were the early sign posts inscribed with the nearest town and distance, but now redundant, many have been uprooted and used as gate posts.

What makes this stoop special is it association with Robin Hood and a local story which has given it the name Robin Hood's Stoop. Purport-edly this is the site where Robin

Robin Hood's Stoop

Hood and Little John once stood and shot a legendary arrow to land in Hathersage churchyard. As the distance is in excess of one mile this was quite an achievement.

Follow the lane until reaching Offerton Hall (4), one of the ancient homes of the powerful, ubiquitous, land-owning Eyre clan who provided an abundant supply, of quixotic material at a time when Gothic tales of mystery and romance were in fashion.

One tale tells how Robert and Elizabeth Eyre of Highlow Hall, (Highlow seems a contradiction of terms but low is actually hlaw meaning a high hill) built a house for each of their seven sons, positioned within sight of each other around Hathersage so that the family could use a form of semaphore to communicate with each other.

But the Eyre legends go way back. Apparently, the first Eyre was named Truelove and he saved William the Conqueror's life at the Battle of Hastings when he released the king's visor and gave him air. The near asphyxiated king exclaimed 'Truelove you have shown me and henceforth thou shalt be known as Air, for thou hast given me air.' It's a good story but it has two major flaws. Truelove is an English name of a later period and the Normans did not have helmets with visors.

But that's not all. Again at the Battle of Hastings, Truelove aka Air, corrupted over the years to Eyre, lost a leg, probably hacked off by some irate Saxon in retribution for restoring the King's air supply. When William heard about this, as a reward he is said to have granted Air the crest of the severed leg, and land in Derbyshire. Truelove aka Eyre apparently arrived at Hope and as he looked round, he declared, – 'The king has given me hope and this area shall be called Hope from now on.'

The lane goes round the buildings, then look for the footpath sign on your right after the last house. Go through the gate and continue along the footpath to the River Derwent (5) where you will find stepping stones crossing the river. It is not advisable to attempt to cross if the river is in flood, in which case, walk downstream to Leadmill Bridge and retrace the outwards route back to Hathersage.

The stepping stones that cross the River Derwent here, mark the ancient crossing of several packhorse routes.

Having crossed the river, once on the other side turn right with the river on your right. After 500 yards, leave the riverside and follow the path to the far corner of the field to reach the A6187, Castleton Road (6). Cross the road and climb the stile on the far side. Follow the path, crossing the railway line carefully, then bear half-right in the field beyond to walk up to Jagger's Lane (7).

This is another reference to an old packhorse route. A convoy of such horses was known as a 'Jagg' and the men who drove them were 'Jaggers'.

Turn right along Jagger's Lane as it descends into the centre of Hathersage where you will join the main road.

Hathersage was once a major centre for brass buttons, needle and wire making and home to England's first needle making factory in the 1560s.

Turn left and walk along the Main Road passing the George Hotel on your left.

The present building dates from the 1500s but there has been an inn on this site since at least the 15th century. It would originally have been an ale house serving the 'jaggers' along the packhorse trail between Castleton and Sheffield.

Continue until reaching the post office, then turn left into Besom Lane (8).

A besom is a broomstick, the type traditionally associated with witches, so there is every likelihood that this is where they were once made.

Pass the National Westminster Bank on your right and continue until reaching Baulk Lane. Turn left then after 100 yards take the footpath on your right leading towards the church. On reaching the churchyard, aim for the church porch.

The old gravestone in the church porch

In the church porch is an old gravestone bearing the initials LJ. This burial slab was discovered beneath the church's flagstone floor in 1851 and is believed to date from the 14th century. It is understood to have been used to mark the grave of Little John.

Little John's grave

Little John's grave (GR 234817) is opposite the porch. It's a simple earth mound, surrounded by a low enclosure of metal railings erected by the Ancient Order of Foresters in 1929, and marked by three stone slabs. The current headstone informs the reader that 'Here Lies Buried Little John, The Friend & Lieutenant of Robin Hood. He died in a cottage, (now destroyed) to the east of the churchyard.'

The grave was opened in 1728 and bones of an enormous size were found. Around the same time, Little John's bow and cap which had been hung in the chancel of Hathersage church, in keeping with his last wish, were taken for safe keeping to Cannon Hall, Cawthorne near Barnsley from where they have since been removed.

The second time the grave was opened, in 1784, a thigh bone, 32" long was exhumed and put on display by Captain Shuttleworth, brother of the local squire, but the Captain decided that the bone was a source of bad luck and gave it to the parish clerk to arrange for it to be re-buried.

Recent research by Prof. Brian Robinson claims that Little John's grave is actually the site of the official measure of the Hathersage village perch - a unit of measurement which was used during the Middle Ages - standardised as 198 inches. The length of the local perch was settled by some pretty arbitrary methods in those days, one of which involved the use of 16 men as they left the village church at the end of a Sunday service. They were stood in a row, foot to foot behind each other, the total length of their feet being designated as the length of the local perch.

Leave the churchyard by the Lychgate and turn right down Church Bank. The ancient centre of the village was in this area above the church and on a knoll next to it there is an earthwork called Camp Green, which is probably Danish in origin. Follow the road as it turns right to become School Lane. This was one of the old roads leading from Derbyshire into Sheffield, and it's around here that Little John's Cottage (9) stood at the east end of the church, overlooking the valley of the Hood Brook.

Next to the village school you will find a pub called The Scotsman's Pack that has a pleasant terrace by the side of the Dale Brook where you can sit out on a fine day.

Although the present building dates from 1900, traces of a much older building have been found within the Scotsman's Pack. For centuries it was a regular stopping place for the travelling drapers or packmen from Scotland who visited every farm and village in the area offering their goods – thus the name.

But what makes this inn special is that they claim to own Little John's chair. As you would expect it's big – the back is 5ft (1.5m) high, the seat 2ft (60cm) across but very unlikely to be ancient. According to the inscription on the brass plaque, it was won in a wager by Major G Lucus, Manchester Regiment from Lieut. A Sunderland MC, Royal Tank Regiment in 1950, and presented to the Scotsman's Pack by Mrs N Lucas in October 1960.

Above the chair hangs a rather interesting framed poem. It's called 'Little John's Grave':

The Scotsman's Pack was full that night, the talk flowed fast and free
And wondrous tales were brought to light by all that company

The Scotsman's Pack claim to have Little John's chair

A sun burnt hiker told the tale, oh how mid ice and snow
And shrouding fog and driving hail 'Cross Kinder he did go

Another told how all alone, he'd gone down Eldon Hole
And come up close to Bolsterstone, or else at Stanage Pole

An aged man did then relate how on the stroke of ten
A ghost hopped o'er the churchyard gate and walked the world
*   again*
'Twas Little John himself' said he, and then began to chime
The hour of ten. Regretfully the landlord shouted 'Time'.

The lights were dimmed and then arose a figure strange I ween
Full seven feet high from head to toes and dressed in Lincoln
*   Green*

He spoke in deep sepulchral tones 'My name is Little John;
Beneath these yews they laid my bones, my life on earth is gone

A big stone at my head and feet, I sleep in earthly bed
But the lies you fellows told to-neet are enough to wake the dead.'

'Gadzooks, i'faith, and by my soul, my slumbers you did break
I could draw the long-bow well myself, but you chaps take the cake.'

And with these words he floated out before their very eyes
So tipplers mind what you're about and in your tales be wise

And as you drink the spirits down and your spirits start to soar
Beware lest all the yarns you spin bring spirits back once more.

Leave the Scotsman's Pack (9) and proceed down the hill to meet the
A6187 road. Turn right and walk straight through the village. Over on
your left is Station Road and standing back on the corner of Station
Road and Mill Lane is the three storey Little John Hotel (10).

This is a traditional Victorian pub; note the original stained glass
windows. It was originally called the Butcher's Arms, then the Drum
and Monkey, then with the arrival of the railways it changed its name
again to the Station Hotel to attract new custom. In the 1940s it was

renamed the Little John Hotel, and now, in keeping with the Robin Hood legend, according to their website they have a dungeon and a Sheriffs room. And remember the old ditty;-

> *You gentlemen and yeoman good*
> *Come in and drink with Robin Hood*
> *If Robin Hood has been and gone*
> *Come in and drink with Little John*

Walk straight through the village until passing under the railway bridge (11). Turn left at an acute angle onto the footpath. Walk to the left of the old barn, then cross the field towards the far right-hand corner. Go through the stile and over the stream to Dore Lane (12). Turn right and walk round the corner where, at the entrance drive to Nether Hall, you leave Dore Lane, cross the stile and walk down the track.

Keep to the right hand side of the first field, crossing the stile at the end, ignoring the track to the right near the end of the first field which goes to a farm. Stay on the right side of the second field to reach the road at Leadmill Bridge (13). Turn right over the bridge and you come to the Plough Inn which is the start/end of this walk.

Statue of Little John

Walk 14: Hathersage and Robin Hood's Cave

People flock to Hathersage to see the grave of Little John, Robin Hood's right hand man, yet there is much more to see. Our walk will start by the vicarage, where Charlotte Brontë stayed in 1845, and on the way we'll pass North Lees Hall, Charlotte's inspiration for Thornfield in her novel Jane Eyre. This invigorating walk has good views but lots of ascents and descents, and can be windy on the exposed tops as it takes you to Robin Hood's Cave. For refreshment there's The Little John Hotel, and The Scotsman's Pack where you'll find a chair alleged to have belonged to Little John.

Distance	4¾ miles (7.70)
Starting point	Hathersage Parish Church
How to get there	Hathersage sits along the main A6187 Sheffield to Castleton road east of the Hope Valley
Parking	Hathersage sits along the main A6187 Sheffield to Castleton road east of the Hope Valley
Map	Ordnance Survey OS Explorer OL1 and OL24
Map reference	GR 234818

The Robin Hood connection
Places bearing the name Robin Hood and his loyal sidekick Little John are abundant in the Derbyshire Peak District, especially around Hathersage, the alleged birth and burial place of Little John. The hills and valleys around here would have echoed to the sound of Robin Hood's hunting horn, and this hidden cave high on Stanage Edge

would have made a secure hideout and great look out post for Robin and his followers.

The Walk

Our walk begins at Hathersage Parish Church dedicated to St Michael, one of the Archangels or chief angels.

It is believed that a Celtic missionary monk first brought Christianity to Hathersage in the 7th century, and built a small cell on the site of the present church. There has certainly been a church here since 1125,

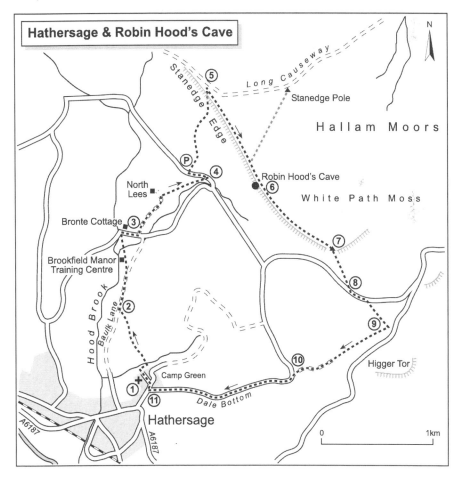

Hathersage & Robin Hood's Cave

and the present building dates from 1381AD. It's an interesting church and a visit is highly recommended, but apart from the 600 year old gravestone in the porch, there is no reference to Little John; his great bow, arrows, some chain armour and a green cap that were once there have since disappeared. (For details of Little John and his grave see Walk 13).

Leave Little John's grave and take the path between the church and the vicarage on your left.

Charlotte Brontë stayed at Hathersage Vicarage with her friend, Elen Nussey,during the summer of 1845, and drew her inspiration for one of her best-loved stories, Jane Eyre from the neighbourhood. Hathersage became Morton , the name of the landlord of The George Hotel.

Leave the churchyard (1), turn right into the parking area and look for the public footpath sign and stile beside a metal farm gate on your left. Cross and walk on a grass path to a marker post with yellow arrows. Turn left and descend the field, crossing Hood Brook at the bottom.

Hood Brook runs through Hathersage and used to power the wire-drawing mills in the town. Hathersage became home to England's first

Hathersage Vicarage

needle making factory in the 1560s and remained a major centre for metalwork and wire drawing until the 19th century. In the 1800s Hathersage was a smoky, dust-laden place. Its chief industries wire drawing and the manufacture of needles and pins. The worst job was grinding points on needles, work which took years off the operators lives.

Ascend the next field keeping the hedge line on your left. The path forks part way up (2), take the left fork which after 300m (¼ mile) will reach Baulk Lane. Turn right and walk along Baulk Lane. Take the footpath on your left as the route then passes through the grounds of Brookfield Manor Training

The area would have echoed to the sound of Robin Hood's hunting horn

Centre to enter a narrow walled path, which eventually comes out on Birley Lane opposite Brontë Cottage. Turn right then left up the drive to North Lees Hall (3).

Over the years, many writers have been inspired by this Elizabethan Hall's desolation set in the folds of the hills above Hathersage, but by far the most famous was Charlotte Brontë. North Lees Hall obviously fired her fertile imagination and made an easy adaptation to her fictitious Thornfield Hall, home of Mr Edward Rochester, where Jane Eyre became governess. Even the name has been adopted from North Lees: 'Thorn' is an anagram of 'north', and 'field' is derived from 'lee', a medieval word for pasture. And if that wasn't proof enough, Charlotte's name for her heroine was taken directly from the residents of North Lees Hall at the time, the Eyres. Three other local properties also featured in Jane Eyre; Brookfield Manor becomes Vale Hall, Moorseats became Moor House, home of the Rivers family where her heroine Jane Eyre sheltered from a snow storm after fleeing from Thornfield, and Fox House (see Walk 15) is thought to have been the model for White Cross.

It's very likely that Charlotte saw North Lees through the same eyes as Jane Eyre who, in the novel, describes her first impression of Thornfield Hall. 'I looked up and surveyed the front of the mansion. It was three storeys high, of proportions not vast, though considerable: a gentleman's manor house, not a nobleman's seat with battlements round the top gave it a picturesque look.'

Other features of the Hall can be readily identified in the novel, such as the view from the roof and the battlemented façade. 'Leaning over the battlements and looking far down, I surveyed the grounds laid out like a map...the road, the tranquil hills, all reposing in the Autumn day's sun; the horizon bounded by a propitious sky, azure, marbled with pearly white. No feature in the scene was extraordinary but all was pleasing.'

The same accurate description of North Lees Hall, and its environs could be made today, and there's also the ruins of a chapel of pre-Reformation date, which may have been 'the quiet and humble temple' where Jane Eyre and Edward Rochester were to be married.

Another coincidence –Agnes Ashurst, a previous elderly resident of North Lees Hall is reputed to have gone mad and been confined to a

North Lees Hall, Hathersage, the inspiration for Thornfield Hall in 'Jane Eyre'

room on the second floor. She later perished in a fire – a similar fate to that of Edward Rochester's wife.

The estate passed to the Peak National Park Authority in 1971 and since 1988, it has been leased to the Vivat Trust and converted into holiday accommodation.

Passing through the farmyard of North Lees, follow the path upwards towards Stanage Edge, which is now ahead. Go up through the trees by a stream to emerge at the road (4). Turn left, then right into the Hollins Bank Car Park. Follow the road round to the public toilets, then turn right just before them onto a path known as Jacob's ladder that heads up through scattered pines, going through a gate into Stanage Plantation. Leave the wood on the far side, but stay on the path as you ascend on the stone path to climb through a weakness in the crags to reach the top of Stanage Edge (5).

On the top, turn right and follow the path along the edge of White Path Moss. The views are superb and as this is the finest training ground for rock climbers in the country, you might see action on the rocks too. After 1 km (½ mile) on your right you will arrive at the grit stone balcony cut into the edge known as Robin Hood's Cave (SK 244837).

As well as Robin Hood's Cave, Robin Hood has lent his name to a number of local rock-climbing routes like Robin Hood's Cave Gully, Robin Hood's Crack and Robin Hood's Chockstone Chimney. Robin Hood's cave is half way up Robin Hood's Gully. It's a natural grit stone balcony cut into the edge, a fissure in the granite crags in the escarpment of Stanage Edge, with wonderful views across the Derwent Valley. It's well known amongst the climbing fraternity and makes a fantastic picnic spot.

The Rev. M.F. H Hulbert, former vicar of Hathersage claimed in his booklet 'Little John of Hathersage' that:

Hikers can pass within a few feet above and below it in hundreds every summer weekend and never know of its existence. The series of interconnecting caves and passages are very well concealed. They can be reached from the top and come out half way down the face of the cliff giving panoramic views for miles to the south and west. Pools of water can always be found nearby so that anyone in hiding could survive for long periods, and the formation of the caves means they could easily be defended by one man against a large number of attackers. In just such a place, an outlaw might hide for months undetected, if the need arose.

Continue along the edge until reaching the trig point (7). Turn right just before it on a path descending to the road (8). Turn left and walk along the road looking for a stile on the right. Cross and follow the footpath towards a second road, but thirty yards before it (9), turn right and follow the grass path which initially runs parallel with the road. Continue right to the bottom where you emerge on a bend in a road (10). Turn left and continue down the lane. This is Dale Bottom and after half a mile you will reach the houses on the outskirts of Hathersage. The road merges into School Lane (11) with The Scotsman's Pack on your left. Ascend the road opposite to return to the church or follow the road through to the main road and the centre of Hathersage which is the start/end of this walk.

Robin Hood's Cave

Walk 15: Robin Hood's Well and Little John's Well, Longshaw Estate

This walk takes you through an outstanding area of dramatic moorland, stands of relict woodland and lush farmland providing excellent walking with dramatic views and iconic sites. The Longshaw estate of 1,086 acres is one of the finest open spaces owned by the National Trust, renowned for its oak woods with their scattered ancient relics. The former shooting estate of the Duke of Rutland, our walk continues to Padley and the little chapel where an annual service is held to commemorate the Padley martyrs. After your walk you might like to visit Fox House Inn. Originally a shepherd's cottage built about 1773, its isolated position is believed to be the model for White Cross in Charlotte Brontë's *Jane Eyre*.

The Robin Hood connection
Robin Hood's Well (GR 267799) and Little John's Well (GR 266794) were used for centuries by travellers crossing the moors on what is

Distance	4¼ miles (6.90km)
Starting point	Longshaw Estate Visitor Centre Car Park
How to get there	Take the A625 from Sheffield. This becomes the A6187 Hathersage Road. At Fox House Inn, branch left along the Owler Bar Road and after a hundred yards turn right into the Longshaw Estate Car Park
Parking	Park in the car park of the Longshaw Estate Visitor Centre off the B6187 (there is a charge), or the car park of the Fox House Inn if you are using the facilities
Map	Ordnance Survey OS Explorer OL1 and OL24
Map reference	GR 267801

now the Longshaw Estate, between Sheffield and Hathersage. Not far from here, according to the 17th century writer Elias Ashmole, is the site of Robin Hoods two Pricks.

The Walk

Before leaving the Longshaw estate car park (1), with your back to the entrance, turn left and, on the edge of the car park, you will find the remains of several small brooks fed from a spring known as Robin Hood's well. It's rather disappointing that there is no gushing spring to see. The only indication of its location is the grid reference.

Follow the well signed path from the car park downhill to the Visitor Centre. At a T-junction turn right if you wish to visit the Visitor Centre with shop, café, toilets and information centre, or at the fork turn left into the woodland along

Robin Hood's Well in the middle of an ancient oak wood

the broad path. At the end of the trees (2) pass through a gate and continue ahead across an open area. After 250m, on your right you will pass a heap of loose stones where Little John's Well used to bubble up.

Continue until the path forks. Bear left to reach the A6187 (3).Turn right until, after a few yards, meeting its junction with the A625 and B6054. Head across to the large white gate and National Trust sign for White Edge Moor.

Walk along a track towards White Edge Lodge, ignoring the left fork just before the Lodge (4). After passing the Lodge, the rough track becomes grassy. Keep ahead to reach a T-junction with the A625 (5).

Cross over the road and turn left, then right in 10 metres through a gate back onto the Longshaw Estate, to follow a broad track north. When the track disappears into woodland take the stile on the left.

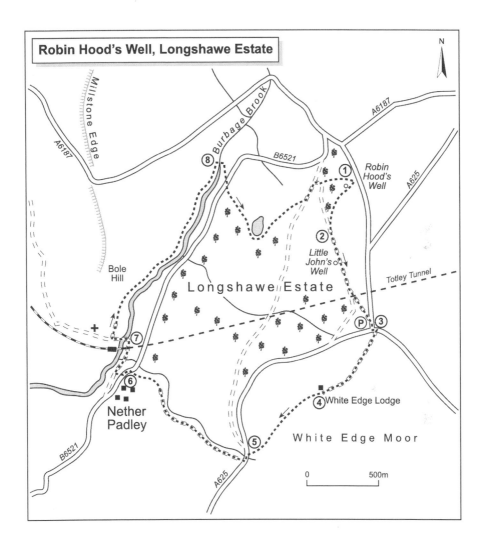

Climb this and follow the path, which is paved at first. The path moves slightly away from a wall on the right and can become a little boggy down towards Oaks Wood, at the head of a valley. Bear to the right, at first, without the aid of a visible path down into the valley, which soon starts to drop down steeply and involves a little bit of scrambling over rocks with a stream on your left. At the bottom of the hill you reach the B6521 Fox House to Grindleford road (6).

Three quarters of a mile down this road is Grindleford Bridge near where, according to Elias Ashmole born in 1617, there is an item called Robin Hood's Two Pricks. Unfortunately there seems to be no indication where or what these 'pricks' are. The mid seventeenth century manuscript, now at Oxford translates to read 'Little John lyes buried in Hathersage Church yard within three miles of Castleton in High Peake, with one stone set up at his head and another at his feet, but a large distance between them. They say a part of his bow hangs up in the said church. Near Grindleford Bridge are Robin Hoods 2 Pricks.'

The ancient handwritten extract from Elias Ashmole's manuscript

Turn left along the B6521 road, then right in 10 metres to join a steep downhill surfaced path, which leads down to Grindleford Station. Turn right at the T-junction to pass the café on your right and cross over the railway line (7). Look over to your right.

The Totley tunnel begins just after this crossing taking the Sheffield bound trains deep under the moors to emerge at Totley, Sheffield. It was dug in the 1890s and at 6,230 yards (5.694m) is one of the longest railway tunnels in Britain.

When the surfaced road ends, continue along a rough track over a stream and past Padley Mill.

Although now a private house, Padley Mill was once a corn mill and later a saw mill, powered by the Burbage Brook on its way to the Derwent.

At a T-junction of tracks, turn right. It is worthwhile making a short detour to visit Padley Chapel first, so continue straight ahead, passing Grindleford station.

Only a few stone now remain of the 15th century Padley Hall, near Grindleford, built by a family called Padley somewhere between 1350 and 1400. In the 16th century Padley was under the control of the Fitzherberts of Norbury. They were staunch Catholics, an allegiance which carried considerable risks in the reign of Elizabeth I when Catholics were suffering for their faith. On 12th July, 1588, the hall was raided and two priests, Robert Ludlam and Richard Garlick, were hauled from their hiding place in the chimney. Their only crime was heresy. They were arrested, tried and sentenced to be hanged, drawn and quartered at Derby. For his part, Sir Thomas Fitzherbert was imprisoned and died in the Tower of London in 1591.

The hall later fell into ruins and at one time it was even used as a cow-shed, but in 1933 the Roman Catholic Diocese of Nottingham

Longshaw House

purchased the simple barn-like structure which is the gatehouse and restored it as a chapel and shrine to the two Padley martyrs. Each year the terrible persecution of these two priests is commemorated at an annual pilgrimage at Padley Chapel on the Thursday nearest July 12th.

Return to the point where the track branches to the left and head uphill. When the track ends pass through a gate into Padley Gorge. Continue climbing up into woodland through the gorge, walking close to Burbage Brook. Pass through a gate at the end of the woodland into a delightful open area, which is popular with families, and after 200m cross a footbridge over Burbage Brook (8) and continue to head uphill to a gate onto the B6521 road.

Turn right, then left in 10 metres through a gate. Follow the path to pass through another gate and skirt around the edge of the lake before it bends to the left towards Longshaw Lodge on the Longshaw Estate Trail. Pass through another gate and when you are faced with a choice of three gates negotiate the gate to the left, which leads to the National Trust Visitor Centre, and next to it Longshaw House, the original shooting lodge of the Duke of Rutland.

The National Trust has maintained the 1600 acre Longshaw estate since the early 1970s. It was once part of a much larger estate owned by the Dukes of Rutland, which was sold and broken up in 1931. Longshaw Lodge, a Grade II listed building, was built in 1827 as a shooting lodge and amongst the guests who have stayed there were George V and the Duke of Wellington. For a while, the lodge was converted into a military hospital, then after the wars was let to the Holiday Fellowship as a guest house, but in 1969 it was converted into private flats. Next to Longshaw Lodge is the focal point for the estate, the National Trust Visitor Centre open June to September daily, winter weekends and Bank Holidays. In the meadow below the lodge the country's longest established sheepdog trials, which first took place in 1898, are held every first week in September.

Turn left in front of the Visitor Centre, then right at a T-junction. In 20 metres turn left at a T-junction to return to the car park, which is the start/end of this walk.

Walk 16: Robin Hood's Cross – Hope – Bradwell

Hope has always been a strategic spot with the remains of the Roman fort of Navio less than a mile east. The prehistoric track-way known as the Portway came through Hope, a north-south trading route through the heart of the Peak District that once connected important trading settlements and sites such as the Celtic hill fort at Mam Tor. Many of these ancient routes later developed into packhorse trails and salt routes. By the time of the Domesday Book, Hope was an important village within the Royal Forest of the Peak – St Peter's Church was once the main church, within the Royal Forest, with its parish stretching as far as Tideswell and Buxton.

To the north east is Win Hill which stands at 1,523ft, and to the north west is Lose Hill, its slightly taller neighbour. According to legend, in the 7th century, the army of King Edwin of Northumbria (Edwin is buried at Edwinstowe – see walk 4) camped on Win Hill in preparation for a battle with the forces of King Cuicholm of Wessex, who were encamped on Lose Hill across the valley of the River Noe. The next day the battle ensued and the fighting was so ferocious that the waters of the River Noe ran red with blood. King Edwin was victorious, hence

Distance	5¼ miles (8.50km)
Starting point	Hope beside the parish church
How to get there	Hope straddles the B6187 road between Castleton and Hathersage
Parking	The main car park in the centre of Hope next to the Woodroffe Arms
Map	Ordnance Survey OS Explorer OL1 and OL24
Map reference	GR 171835

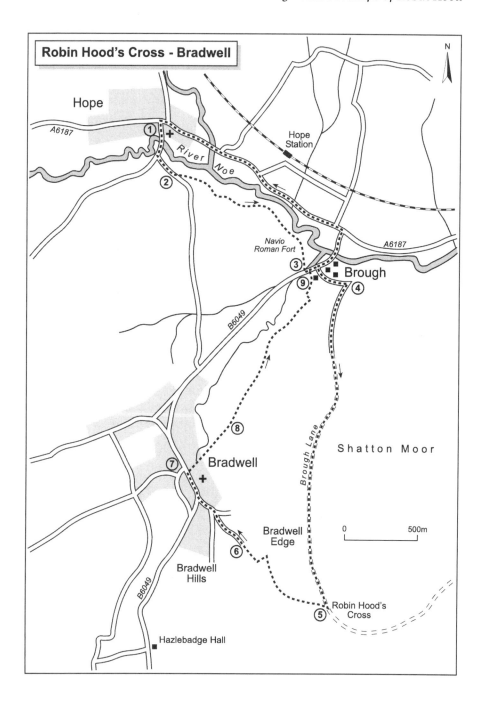

the names of win and lose hill. A more mundane explanation, given by etymologists, is that the name Win Hill means hill of bilberries, while Lose Hill means hill of pigs.

The Robin Hood connection

In the olden days every boundary was traditionally identified by a name, a marker stone or a wayside cross. A 1319 document refers to a medieval wayside cross that stood on an old packhorse route, called the Portway, three miles west of Hathersage. It marked the junction of three parish boundaries, and was named Robin Crosse (GR 184802), making it one of the earliest places recorded. These crosses had a double meaning. They were where itinerate priests and monks would preach when in the area, and on the high-road the cross was frequently placed to deter highwaymen, and restrain other predators, in the same way that in the market place, the market cross was a signal for upright intentions and fair dealings.

By the mid 18th century, the packhorse routes that had been the main highways were being replaced by turnpike roads, a term which stems from the practice of stabbing a pike into the road to stop travellers until they had paid a fee or toll to use that stretch. The toll was used to maintain the roads. As the wayside crosses were no longer of any use, most have now disappeared. Thrifty farmers utilised them as gate posts but the base stone of Robin Hood's Cross, although still marked on ordnance survey maps, is now built into the wall on Bradwell Edge.

The Walk

Leave the car park (1) and turn right walking to the Woodroffe Arms, named after an influential local family who once held the position of the King's Foresters of the Peak.

Woodroffes pre-eminence dates back to the mid 1400s when they distinguished themselves fighting for Edward IV and were granted the right to bear arms.

Forest officials who supervised the royal hunting ground, which once spread across much of the High Peak, would not have been Robin Hood's favourite people. The Lay of Buckstone is a Derbyshire ballad

The Woodroffe Arms named after the King's Foresters of the Peak

of the High Peak, in which a fight takes place between Robin Hood and keepers of the Peak Forest. It mentions the men marching along beneath the Archer's Wall. In a 1797 map of the ancient Forest of the Peak, I traced this old wall, which is still a boundary on Combes Moss, and although it is named the Archer's Wall on the map, the length is traditionally called Robin Hood's Marks.

Inside the church of St Peter, once the main church within the royal forest, are two 13th/14th century coffin stones of former Forest huntsmen and several others are set in the floor. The church is normally locked but in the churchyard is the shaft of a carved Saxon cross, and look up at the display of grotesque gargoyles projecting rain water from the roof.

Walk down Pindale Road between the Woodroffe Arms and the church of St Peter, then branch left along Forres road, looking for a stile beside a seat on your left (2). Cross the stile and follow the path across fields and stiles until arriving at the site of the Roman Fort of Navio (3). It's an atmospheric place, although today only the embankments of the fort walls around the flat central area are left. It requires imagination to picture the Roman fort that stood here.

The Romans reached lowland Derbyshire in 47AD. They conquered the Coritani tribe but found the Brigantes, who inhabited the north of Derbyshire and the Peak District, harder to crush. But it was only a matter of time. They build their fort at Brough-on-Noe on a piece of high ground, in the angle of the River Noe and the Bradwell Brook, and called it Navio which means place by the river.

They needed to take control of this area because of one valuable commodity – lead. Large quantities of lead were mined throughout the Peak District, and lead ore often contained large quantities of silver, so the Peak lead mines would have come under the direct supervision of the Imperial Treasury of Rome. Unfortunately Derbyshire lead contained very little silver, which must have been a great disappointment to the treasury officials, who quickly leased the mines to civil

The view from Navio over Brough to the summit of Robin Hood's Cross

contractors who formed the Societas Lutudarum or Lutudarum Company. Several stamped pigs of lead have been found which carry the name of the company with the cast inscription SOCIORVM LVTVD BRIT. EX. ARG LVTVD which translates as 'The Luatudarum Company, British silver-free lead'.

Leave the fort site and descend the field for just 200m to emerge through a kissing gate onto the B6049 Stretfield Road. This forms part of the Roman road Baltham Gate, which ran from Navio through the Bradwell valley. After crossing the stone bridge, take the first right beside an old barn, to walk along Brough Lane on a steep ascent (4). The route turns into a stony track as you continue ascending and there are great views of Bradwell to your right. Pass the entrance to Ellmore Hill Farm on your left as you continue along the track. Nearing a hill on your right, you come to a metal farm gate across the track.

Here is the site of Robin Hood's Cross (GR 184802) but evidence of the cross is hard to find today. It's built into the wall on Bradwell Edge not far from its original site.

Turn right over the stone step stile just before the gate. Continue on a grass path, keeping the wall to your left, and go through an opening into the next field, then through another opening (5). You are now looking down on the village of Bradwell as you start to descend the hillside of Bradwell Edge on a steep, narrow path with a wall on your left.

Continue on the long, steep descent to a gate at the bottom. You will emerge onto Edge Lane (6). Continue descending, following the narrow road into Bradwell .

Today Bradwell is a historic village of narrow streets and traditional buildings. It's a quiet backwater, yet until recently there were six factories in the village producing what is known as the 'Bradder Bowler'. Worn by the lead miners, the felt protected the head and the brim was used to hold a candle.

Continue through Bradwell until reaching the church. Across the road is a cottage with an inscription mounted on the wall, as this was the childhood home of Samuel Fox.

Samuel Fox was born in this cottage in June 1815. He served an apprenticeship in the wire industry in Hathersage, before launching into business on his own. He experimented with the flexibility of steel wire and soon his Paragon Frame Umbrella became a best seller. He also provided telegraph wires, cable rods and winding ropes for mine shafts, providing employment for many needy Bradwellians, and anonymously providing for many more. When he died on 26th February, 1887, his company employed 2,000 workers - one hundred years later it employed 6,000.

Just past the church is a small bridge over the stream (7). Turn right just before the bridge, and walk 150 yards along the lane to a public footpath sign on the right. Follow it, and you soon go through an opening into a field (8), then through a series of fields. When the Romans left, Bradwell became a tribal boundary and its people built Grey Ditch across the dale to defend the limestone plateau from the north.

As you are nearing Brough, your path turns left for 45 yards then right to emerge at a road junction with Brough Lane and Balham Gate at Brough (9). Just before the main road look out for St Anne's Well, dating from 1859. At the traffic lights in Brough, turn left to walk back on the pavement into Hope which is the start/end of this walk.

Walk 17: The Norman Castle at Castleton

Castleton is one of the Peak District's premier tourist destinations, renowned for its caverns and ancient castle, named Peveril Castle after its builder, and made famous by Sir Walter Scott's *Peveril of the Peak*. The town nestles at the feet of the castle from which its name is derived. The main tower, or keep, which added so much to the symbolic function of Peveril Castle was built between 1155- 76 at a cost of less than £200. It is now the only surviving example of a Norman castle in the county and one of the best preserved in Britain. The £100 spent on its upkeep by King John between 1205 and 1212 was obviously well spent. As well as the shell of the keep, much of the curtain wall survives, and within it the foundations of other buildings can be traced making the climb up to Peveril Castle well worth while.

The other great attraction that draws thousands of visitors annually are the Castleton Caverns, a mixture of natural caves, early tunnelling accomplished with sheer muscle power, and modern innovation. Our walk completes a circuit of the four main cavern systems, ending with a stunning descent down Winnat's Pass and back to the town.

Sir Arthur Conan-Doyle, creator of Sherlock Holmes, the most famous detective in English literature, stayed near Castleton and was inspired to write, "All this country is hollow. Could you strike it with some gigantic hammer it would boom like a drum, or possibly cave in altogether and expose some huge subterranean sea. A great sea there must surely be, for on all sides the streams run into the mountain itself never to reappear. There are gaps everywhere amid the rocks, and when you pass through them you find yourself in great caverns, which wind down into the bowels of the earth."

The Robin Hood connection
Under the Saxon rule of Edward the Confessor small villages prospered, then the Normans invaded and conquered, and William 1, better known as the Conqueror, granted land and property to his followers. When two Norman earls attempted to take over their

Distance	3¾ miles (6km)
Starting point	Castleton
How to get there	Castleton sits astride the A6187 road 1¼ miles from Hope
Parking	Park in the pay and display car park by the side of the museum in the heart of the town
Map	Ordnance Survey OS Explorer OL1 and OL24
Map reference	GR 150830

recently granted Northumbrian estates, they were murdered, and this was the start of the Harrying of the North, the most fearful act of genocide in English history. William hastily sent his storm troopers North in an act of retribution, in which 100,000 people perished and hundreds of settlements were laid waste.

We have a first hand account of the terrors of those years from the chronicler Orderic Vitalis:

'It was terrible to see rotting corpses covered in multitudes of worms in the silent dwellings and deserted street and roads with the atmosphere made foul by the stench of purification. Nobody remained to bury the corpses.....Nothing moved in the scorched ruins of villages but the packs of wolves and wild dogs which tore apart the human corpses.'

In the Derbyshire Chapters of the Domesday Book one phrase that crops up constantly is 'wasta est' meaning it is waste. The entry for this area states simply: 'All Longdendale is waste; woodland, unpastured, fit for hunting'. The value of this 72 square mile area before 1066 had been 40 shillings (£2). It was now a worthless waste and became part of the 40 square mile Royal Forest of the Peak – a hunting ground with deer, wild boar, brown bear and wolf, set aside for the king and his cronies.

To administer this and control all hunting, William gave the site to his illegitimate son William Peveril, son of Maud, daughter of a Saxon nobleman, Ingelric, Earl of Essex. She later married Ranulph Peveril of Hatfield Peveril, Essex, and William adopted the surname of the family into which his mother married.

Standing on the summit of a small limestone ridge with magnificent views across the Hope Valley was a Saxon fortification, called Castle in the Peak – Alto Pecco Castle or Castel de Pecco. An earth-work wall extended in a half moon formation round the village joined the Castle at each end, and thus the Castle enclosure became Castleton – 'ton' being of Anglo-Saxon origin and meaning 'enclosure'. In 1086 William chose this almost impregnable site to build his Norman castle, declaring its owner's power and status. It was used regularly by kings for the hunting and was also an administrative centre for management of lead mining, which brought huge financial benefits to the Peverils, all ensuing owners and the crown.

The remains of Peveril Castle

William Peveril lived in style at Peveril Castle and, according to tradition, he held a large jousting tournament here – the prize being the hand of his only daughter Mellet in marriage, and her dowry of Whittington Castle in Shropshire. To ensure that she married a man who would be worthy of such an heirloom, invitations were sent out to all the noble knights of the land, and bold and courageous knights came from far and wide to joust for her hand and her dowry. The eventual victor was Guaine de Matz, a knight of Lorraine, and ancestor of the Lords Fitz-Warrine, who, with his maiden shield of silver and peacock crest, vanquished many knights, including a prince of Scotland and a knight of Burgoyne.

William Peveril Jnr inherited the castle on the death of his father in 1114, but the Peverils lost it when they took the wrong side against King Henry II, in 1152. In 1153, Henry II seized Peveril Castle and the castles of Nottingham and Bolsover, which became Royal properties. They changed hands many times after that, usually held by the king and records show that, in 1173, £135 was spent on knights and their servants at Bolsover, Peveril and Nottingham Castles. In 1189 Richard I gave the castle to Prince John, who held it until 1212; so did Robin Hood's feud with John reach Castleton?

The Walk

Leave the car park (1) by the entrance into Cross Street, cross the road and proceed into Castle Street which runs between the Castle Inn and the Church of St Edmund. Although the church was practically rebuilt in 1837, it has Norman foundations and a fine early Norman chancel arch. Like most places of worship, this church has continually evolved as the Norman invaders rebuilt churches to try to suppress local traditions in favour of their own.

Oak Apple Day may have slipped almost unnoticed from our calendars, but the significance of the day is still remembered in Castleton. On the evening of 29th May, crowds flock here to see a celebration that has taken place annually since at least 1749. The main event is a dancing procession through the streets led by 'the King' and his Lady on horse back. Although half the king's apparel is hidden by a huge floral garland, which is really the centre of attention, both the King and Queen wear Stuart costumes. This emphasizes the idea that this ceremony dates back to 1660, to mark the restoration of the monarchy after years of bitter conflict and strict puritan rule during the Civil War. The Stuart restoration was met with a great surge of national enthusiasm and welcomed the return of popular rural sports, customs and celebrations previously banned under the strict puritanical regime of the Parliamentarians.

However, this takes the custom much further back into history, and observers would say that the 'King', covered with a bell-shaped structure like a giant garland looks remarkably like that May Day character 'Jack in the Green'. This was a man who danced inside a wood or basketwork frame covered in an abundance of greenery and flowers that covered him from head to ankles. The visual effect was of a conical bush on feet. Using flowers and greenery in abundance is more in keeping with the earlier pagan fertility rites which have their roots in the worship of the earth, and 'Jack in the Green' is often confused with the so called 'Green Man' depicted in the foliated heads found on many churches. In folklore, there are even claims that Robin Hood, dressed in Lincoln Green, stems from the image of the Green man.

Oak Apple Day appears to have absorbed some of the customs normally associate with May Day. This was the first day of Celtic summer and a prime festival of pastoral England rooted in pagan fertility rites. Whole villages joyfully 'brought in May' – a phrase embracing both the month and the sweet-smelling white hawthorn blossom. Country folks rambled through the green woods on May Eve, returning home as the sun rose, laden with branches of may blossom to deck their homes and welcome summer. The day was spent in merrymaking with maypole dancing and rural sports, but these simple pleasures ceased when England was plunged into Civil War, so was it any wonder that these celebrations were joyfully restored when Charles returned in 1660? May games continued for the whole month to incorporate both celebrations until Oak Apple Day absorbed the old, gradually fading May Day. It was the Victorians that revived May Day in expurgated form. In some areas, May Day became Garland Day. Children dressed up and paraded with their May Garlands made from a mixture of wild and garden flowers fixed to a wooden frame, with a doll – 'the lady' – within. Happily these old traditions like Maypole dancing, although now relatively low key, still take place in many villages.

At the top of Castle Street, past the memorial cross and Market Place, turn right to follow the sign posted riverside walk (2), to arrive at a road named The Stones.

It was here that Randolph Douglas established a museum at his cottage home. Previously a gentleman named Rooke Pennington had collected local artefacts and allowed the public to view them – a sort of early museum, but now Castleton has a museum, next to the car park you used earlier.

Here is the entrance to Peak Cavern which has been given the more unsavoury name of 'The Devil's Arse'. As you approach the cavern, you walk beside the brook which comes from deep inside the cave but, on occasions, this brook becomes an angry, yellow, opaque torrent. 'That,' say the locals, 'Is when the devil is relieving himself.'

Peak Cavern has the largest natural cave entrance in the British Isle, which in previous centuries actually housed a small subterranean community of up to 30 rope makers and their families. Traces of their sunless, stone built, thatched cottages plus stables and an inn can still be seen on the cave walls to the right and the soot from their chimneys is still visible on the roof of the cavern. An engraving, dated 1721, shows the cottages which stood for a further hundred years or so. The last person to live in Peak Cavern was Mary Knight, who died in 1845, but the rope making continued until 1974, when the last rope maker Bert Marrison retired at the age of 89. It is still possible to see the weird, gallows-like uprights and posts, the flying ropes and hanging weights, with adjacent suggestions of vast wheels and curious figures standing out against the darkness.

At the end of The Stones, turn right over a bridge and continue up Goosehill. The road leads into a stony lane, then onto a field path. Follow the field wall with steep hills all around as you approach the head of the valley.

Cross the road, Arthur's Way (3), by Speedwell Cavern at the foot of Winnats Pass.

Speedwell Cavern took its name from the Speedwell Tavern, the public house which is now the gift shop standing just outside the cavern

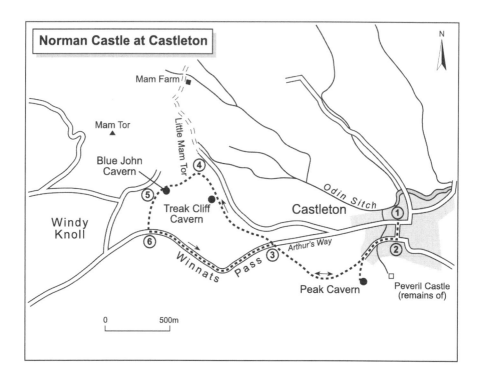

entrance. *Visiting Speedwell Cavern is a memorable and dramatic experience as the subterranean canal excavated by lead mines in the 1770s is navigated by boat.*

Keep straight forward over the field with the wall on your right, to reach a step-stile. Continue, passing to the left of a wood and climbing up Treak Cliff Hill situated on the north side of Winnats Pass.

Within the hill are two well-known caves, Treak Cliff Cavern and Blue John Cavern, the only known source of Blue John in the world. The spar is calcium fluoride coloured by films of oil deposited on the surface of the crystals resulting in a semi-precious stone unique to Derbyshire, named Blue John. It could actually have been from the French name 'Bleu-Jaune' meaning blue-yellow, because it is a rare, discoloured fluorspar varying in colour from dark purple to white via blue and yellow. Treak Cliff Cavern is probably the most attractive of the caverns and has the richest deposits of Blue John. The caverns show a remarkable likeness to Gothic architecture with their rich, variegated natural rock formations, magnificent coloured domes, sparkling cascades of stalagmites, and dazzling pendant stalactites. They have been described as the north of England's finest stalactite caves.

The path passes through the Treak Cliff site, continuing round the hillside in places rather narrow over steep slopes and needing extra care (4).

At a pair of stiles, Mam Tor (Mother Mountain) comes into sight, dominating the view to the right, climbing spectacularly to 1,696ft (517m). It is one of the best known Derbyshire hillforts, once occupied by a Celtic tribe called the Brigantes.

Mam Tor's unstable rock structure, based on the peculiar composition of shale and grit in alternate layers, results in rock falls and the fact that it is seen to be moving has gained it the local name the Shivering mountain. At its base, the A625 used to be the main trans-Pennine route until a rock slide, in 1977, led to its permanent closure to traffic.

Cross the left-hand stile and continue over level grassland to reach Blue John Cavern (5). Go past and continue up and over to reach Winnats Pass (6). Turn left, keeping to the path on the left of the wall in preference to the road.

Winnats Pass is a dramatic limestone gorge climbing steeply out of Castleton. It was once a major entrance into the town carrying the salt route from Cheshire to Yorkshire, and written Wyndeyates, meaning the pass through which the wind sweeps. Drivers used to use the pass purely for the experience, but since the main road over Mam Tor collapsed in 1977, they now do so out of necessity.

Continue down Winnats Pass until reaching Speedwell Cavern where, in the gift shop, you will find an old saddle with a sad story attached.

In April 1758, an eloping couple heading for Peak Forest, which was known as the Gretna Green of England, were murdered in Winnats Pass. When their horses were found wandering near the pass, there was little doubt amongst the locals that something dreadful had befallen

The old saddle with a sad story attached

the young couple. People suspected foul play but with no proof or bodies, no one was ever brought before the courts.

But the dastardly deed had been committed by five murdering miners who paid the price for their crime in a kind of poetic justice. One died within the year, two died in mysterious circumstances, and a third took his own life. The fifth man made a death bed confession to the vicar of Castleton, but it wasn't until a decade after the event that miners unearthed two skeletons – the remains of the two young lovers.

The crime, now practically forgotten, has left us with mute evidence. In a glass case in the Speedwell Cavern gift shop is the lady's side saddle, now only a short distance from the spot where the two young lovers so tragically lost their lives.

Leave the gift shop and return to Castleton which is the start/end of this walk

Walk 18: The Hamlet of Robin Hood and Chatsworth Park – Robin Hood's Seat and Robin Hood's Leap

Chatsworth House, one of Derbyshire's most stately homes is surrounded by 1,000 acres of parkland that originally formed the western boundary of Sherwood Forest. It still has many ancient oak trees as well as herds of roaming deer, so would you be surprised to find, on its northern edge, a hamlet named after the famous outlaw of Sherwood Forest - Robin Hood? This tiny hamlet consists of the

Distance	7 miles (11.35km)
Starting point	The hamlet of Robin Hood
How to get there	To reach Robin Hood from Chesterfield, take the A619 road heading west to Baslow. After six miles, the hamlet of Robin Hood is situated on the right at a right hand junction with the B6050. From Bakewell, take the A619 road to Baslow. Go round two roundabouts as you pass through Baslow and continue on the A619 towards Chesterfield for one mile (1.50km) until reaching the B6050 on your left. The Robin Hood Pub is on the left, set back from the road, as it straddles the junction of the B6050 with the A619
Parking	Turn into the B6050 and park in the Birchin Edge car park adjoining the Robin Hood pub car park
Map	Ordnance Survey OS Explorer OL24
Map reference	GR 281722

Robin Hood Inn, Robin Hood Farm and Robin Hood Plantation, while in the parkland are Robin Hood's Leap and Robin Hood's Seat.

The Robin Hood connection

Robin Hood's Leap is the name of a Derbyshire ballad found in *The Life and Exploits of Robin Hood* (Milner and Sowerby, Halifax 1859) The tale is about a lady called Kitty Ray who lived at Edensor, the estate village in Chatsworth Park. She protected Robin in a delightful love story, so we can assume that Robin spent a considerable amount of times in the vicinity. That's why you will find Robin Hood's Seat, the highest rock above the Old Park Plantation at the southern end of the park. Is this where he and Kitty Ray would sit? There's also a deep gorge in Chatsworth Park that has been given the name Robin Hood's Leap because Robin is said to have leapt over it as he was anxious to get away from the Sheriff's men. As we know, there was no lasting relationship between Robin and Kitty and each went their separate ways.

The Walk

Leave the Birchin Edge car park at Robin Hood (1) and return to the main A619 road. Turn right towards Baslow and, after 50m, you'll see a stile in the stone wall on your left (2) with a finger post indicating Baslow. Cross the road with care.

Once through the stile, take the steps down to a basic wooden footbridge over Heathly Lea Brook, then climbing up the other side, keep right as the path forks. Cross a stony track and continue uphill to a ladder-stile (3).

The path continues uphill, at the back of a series of gritstone crags, known as Dobb Edge, which is a concessionary path. The path is quite easy to follow along the edge of the ridge, down to a step-stile in a high wall. Bear right to follow a grassy hollow way downhill before heading left (there's no distinct path) across the parkland, following the footpath signs to the Hunting Tower (4).

This was previously called Stand Tower and was built in 1582, in order to watch the hounds hunting in the valley below. The woods covering the hillside behind Chatsworth House are known as Stand Wood. Stand

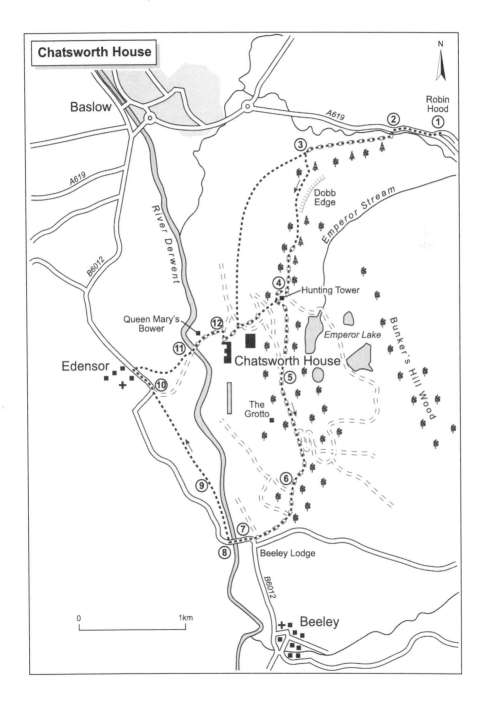

means a place of height for spectators, hence 'grandstand' at a sports arena. The canon at the base of the Hunting Tower came from a ship that fought at the Battle of Trafalgar.

Don't go down the hill to the farmyard/adventure playground. This is the way we will return, but for now keep due south, following the path above Chatsworth House, with the Emperor Lake above on your left.

In 1702, a hill was removed so that the lake could be dug out to act as a reservoir for the impressive fountain called the Emperor, fed by gravity from this reservoir.

The Hunting Tower

Go straight on at a junction (5) and follow the estate road south ignoring all routes off to the left, then the right, until reaching Old Park Plantation, where you will find Robin Hood's Seat, the highest rock above the Old Park Plantation (6). Continue downhill to reach Beeley Lodge and the B6012 road (7). Turn right to walk by the roadside and cross the bridge over the River Derwent.

This is known as One Arch Bridge. The chains hanging from the arch serve the same purpose as a cattle grid you've just crossed – to stop the deer escaping, in this case by swimming out of the park.

Immediately after the bridge, turn right through a metal kissing gate to re-enter Chatsworth Park, which extends to over 450 hectares on both sides of the River Derwent. Follow the grass path, which continues beside the river, and after a short distance you will pass the old water mill (8), built in 1757.

The old water mill used to be a corn mill, powered by the fast flowing water of the River Derwent, and last ground corn in 1952. The building was badly damaged during the gales of 1967, when a huge beech tree fell on top of it.

Follow the riverside path. Over to your right, in the distance and surrounded by trees, is Chatsworth House, undoubtedly one of England's finest stately homes.

In 1549 Bess of Hardwick and her second husband Sir William Cavendish bought the manor of Chatsworth and built a mansion house, which has been added to and changed by subsequent generations of the Cavendish family, whose home it has been for 460 years. It is often referred to as The Palace of the Peak.

At a branch of paths (9), leave the river and veer left, and at the next crossing veer left again heading N.NW for Edensor (10).

Chatsworth House

The Domesday Book records three settlements in the valley on the eastern side of the river, where Chatsworth House now stands – Edensoure, Chetesourde and Langeleie. The latter was last recorded in 1355, which means that, in Robin Hood's days, he would have been familiar with three villages in this area.

The village of Chetesourde seems to have been obliterated at the turn of the 17th century, followed by Edensoure a century later. Over to your left is a solitary cottage in the dip between the road and river, which is all that is left of the original village of Edensoure. The 6th Duke of Devonshire objected to the village being visible from Chatsworth House and had it demolished and rebuilt on its present site around 1740.

To visit Edensor, cross the main B6012 road which runs through Chatsworth Park. You can have refreshment at the Post Office and a visit to St Peters Church, Edensor is recommended. There you can see the monuments and graves of the Cavendish family, but perhaps the most surprising is that of Kathleen Kennedy, sister of John F Kennedy the American President. Kathleen was the wife of William Cavendish, who should have inherited the estate and title of Duke of Devonshire had he not been killed in the Second World War. Four years later, in 1948 at the age of twenty eight, Kathleen was killed in a plane crash.

Leave Edensor and cross the B6012, to take the gravel path which veers right across the park towards the access road to Chatsworth House.

Cross the bridge (11) and note the stone building on your immediate left. This is Queen Mary's Bower, one of the few buildings that date back to the Elizabethan Chatsworth, and named after Mary Queen of Scots.

Mary Stuart first arrived in Derbyshire in March 1565, but it wasn't for a visit. Two months earlier she had been placed under house arrest in the custody of the 6th Earl of Shrewsbury and his wife Bess of Hardwick, who were to remain her captors until 1584. During all those years she was constantly moved around their palatial Derbyshire homes, and was imprisoned five times at Chatsworth House.

The royal status of the captive queen assured her of considerable privileges, except for the own thing she wanted most – freedom to

The Bridge

wander around out of doors. As a slight concession, this single storey structure with blank stone walls was built in the grounds near the River Derwent. It was topped with a flat roof surrounded by a wall broken in places by stone balustrading. The design is rather like a raised play-pen and formed what we would call a roof garden, where the captive Queen could wonder. As a further precautionary step, the whole was surrounded by a moat and entered by a steep flight of stone steps leading to a substantial door, over which are Mary's initials and coat of arms. The design of this moated bower, with its raised garden, allowed Mary to spend considerable time in the open, while still enclosed behind restricting walls with a locked door or gate.

Leave Queen Mary's Bower and walk up to the entrance of Chatsworth House and Chatsworth stables which now house a couple of very nice restaurants and craft shops (12). A few hours spent here is highly recommended.

To continue our walk, cross a cattle grid and pass Chatsworth Farmyard, on your left. Follow the estate road as it bears right up through the woods signed 'Stand Wood Walks'. After about 100 metres, opposite an old building and just before four coloured arrows on a low stone on the left-hand side of the road, leave the road and turn left up a narrow woodland path through the laurels and rhododendrons. Cross another wider track diagonally left and continue up the winding, narrow path, crossing a stream and walking round a large Yew tree to the steps.

Climb the 148 steps to the Hunting Tower (4). Turn left to follow the road round the tower on the track signposted Robin Hood. Isn't this just the kind of place you might expect to encounter the famous outlaw?

Now re-trace your steps. At a crossing of roads turn left on a surfaced road through the woods. After about ½ mile, the road bends right up to a large shed. Keep straight on along a farm track for a few metres, then just before a gateway turn left through the wood. Follow the wall on your right. Cross the high wall stile, turn right then left to follow the wall on your right.

After about 300 metres, and before the wall corner, the path bears left to cross another high stile. Keep straight on up the field to walk along the concessionary path of Dobb Edge (11). Cross the stile in the field corner. Follow the narrow, winding, rocky path as it undulates.

Cross two stiles and after about 400 metres at the end of Dobb Edge, cross a ladder stile. Bear left down hill following the way marked post and crossing a wider track. Go down steps to cross a planked bridge over Heathy Lea Brook then climb the steps to the A619 road. Cross the road and turn right to return to Robin Hood, the start/end of this walk.

Walk 19: The Hamlet of Robin Hood and The Lost Villages

A very popular walk with lots of interest along Birchin Edge. With Curbar and Froggat edges, they form a magnificent long gritstone escarpment which stretches along the eastern rim of the Derwent Valley. This natural wall to the valley is a magnet for rock climbers and offers extensive views for walkers

Distance	4½ miles (7.30km)
Starting point	The hamlet of Robin Hood
How to get there	To reach Robin Hood from Chesterfield, take the A619 road heading west to Baslow. After six miles, the hamlet of Robin Hood is situated on the right at a right hand junction with the B6050. From Bakewell, take the A619 road to Baslow. Go round two roundabouts as you pass through Baslow and continue on the A619 towards Chesterfield for one mile (1.50km) until reaching the B6050 on your left. The Robin Hood Pub is on the left, set back from the road, as it straddles the junction of the B6050 with the A619
Parking	Turn into the B6050 and park in the Birchin Edge car park adjoining the Robin Hood pub car park
Map	Ordnance Survey OS Explorer OL24
Map reference	GR 281722

The Robin Hood connection

The hamlet of Robin Hood is well worth a visit for Robin Hood fans and it's got a pub – rather unsurprisingly called The Robin Hood. This walk also discovers a couple of lost villages that would have been ancient even in Robin's time.

The Walk

Leave the Birchin Edge car park (1) and turn left up the B6050. Pass Robin Hood Farm on your left then leave the road, turning left to walk up the bank to go through a five bar gate.

Keep straight on up the wide steps, following the well-used sand and rock path uphill round to the left, following the garden wall. Pass the nine hole golf course on your left, at the back of the Robin Hood Pub. Ignore the path on the right and continue, ignoring another smaller path on the right, and follow the rocky path below Birchin Edge.

On the edge of Birchin Edge was a town called Leash Fen, which is still marked on maps. A flat 700 acres site, it is now one of the most desolate and least frequented places in Derbyshire and gets it's name from the Old English 'lecc'

A steady climb

meaning stream and 'fenn' a marsh. Little grows there except marsh grasses, some heather and a few scrubby trees, but in the late 1830s, a drainage trench was dug across the middle of the marsh and, in the process, 'many pieces of black oak, squared and cut by some instrument' were found along with some fragments of rude earthenware and coinage. Similar signs of early civilization were later uncovered during excavation for an electricity power line, yet no detailed description or precise location for these finds was ever specified

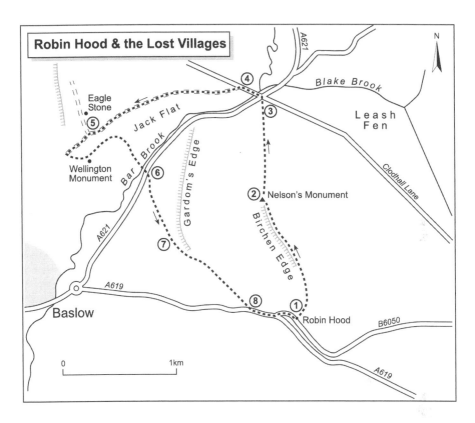

In the fen area early dwelling places or huts would almost certainly have been built on piles, which would tie in with the many pieces of squared black oak found buried, yet no further excavation has been done, so the mystery of Leash Fen lives on. Is this a lost town? Some credence is given to the legend by an ancient rhyme:

> *When Chesterfield was heath and broom, Leash Fen was a market town.*
> *Now Leash Fen is all heath and broom and Chesterfield is a market town.*

Continue along this path and soon you will see Nelson's Monument (2) up to your right, perched on the top of the Edge, 1,000ft above sea level.

Nelson's Monument was erected in 1810, in memory of Admiral Lord Nelson (1758-1805) and the Battle of Trafalgar, in which he died along with over 1,580 fellow sailors. The gritstone shaft is topped with a stone finial ball and each side of the obelisk faces a cardinal point of the compass. The eastern side is inscribed AD Nelson. Died Oct. 21st 1805. On the opposite side, John Brightman the stonemason left his initials. Behind the monument are three large rocks known as the Three Ships. They represent the famous British ships in that battle; their names, Victory, Defiant and Royal Soverin (sic), are carved into each rock.

Continue along the edge to a white pillar known as a trig point or triangulation point.

Trig points were set up by the Ordnance Survey after 1845 on numerous sites in Britain, to enable them to survey the country and hence provide maps. Today trig points are no longer used as aerial and satellite photography provides far more accurate mapping details.

Near the northern end of Birchen Edge the path veers left, away from the edge, and winds its way down through the purple flowering heather, much loved by Derbyshire bees. Very little grows up here, yet over on your left is an area called Gardom's Edge (SK 275735).

This was another Bronze Age settlement, dating from the same era as the better known Stanton Moor. Gardom's Edge, like the previous Leash Fen site is one of a number of small settlements and associated field systems clustered along this gritstone edge between Totley and Beeley. First colonised around 2000BC, they were abandoned by 1,200BC because of land exhaustion resulting from over grazing, soil erosion and increased rainfall. Little activity has taken place in this area over the last 3000 years to destroy the evidence, and these sites afford us a glimpse of a fossilised landscape.

A 1,500ft long strip of the edge is enclosed by the remains of a massive dry stone wall, some 15ft in diameter. It's western edge is formed by the cliffs themselves and a tumbled entrance can be discerned along the southern section of the wall. It is possible that the enclosure served as a corral for stock grazing on the surrounding fields and higher moorland, though its large size and strategic position indicates a more defensive role. It may have served as a proto – hill fort.

Between the enclosure and the moorland to the east are a number of irregular stone walls, which once segregated small plots which could be cross ploughed for cereal cultivation like carbonised barley. Huts, either living quarters or store sheds, would have been erected in the corner of these fields. The inhabitants of Gardom's Edge probably practiced farming, with sheep and cattle rearing being the main activity. The nearby settlement of Swine Sty on Big Moor has produced evidence of a craftsman's workshop where shale jewellery was made. This indicates that, although life must have been hard and basic, there was enough surplus wealth to support a non-agricultural artisan.

As you follow the path north the ground can become very marshy as sedge grasses and rushes take the place of the heather. Continue ahead heading for the road junction of Clodhall Lane and the A621 Sheffield/Baslow Road (3).

Cross the road with care and head directly up the hill towards Curbar, pausing at the quaint old bridge that crosses the Bar Brook. After about 100 yards, go through a gate beside a field gate (4) and follow the track along Eagle stone Flat to the Wellington Monument which you will reach after about ¾ mile.

This cross was erected in 1866 by Mr Wrench, a Baslow doctor, who had previously served as an army surgeon in the Crimean War and India. As the name implies, it is in memory of the Duke of Wellington (1769-1852) of Wellington boot fame and his famous victories, particularly the Battle of Waterloo.

On the southern end of Baslow Edge, behind the monument, is a large rock known as the Eagle Stone. Whichever way you view it, this huge pile of deformed gritstone has none of the characteristic features of an eagle. In fact anything less bird like than a solid clump of rock is hard to imagine until you realise that Eagle is a corruption of Aigle, the Saxon god who could throw stones that no mortal could move. A local tradition was for the young men of Baslow to climb to the top of the Eagle stone to prove their prowess in some kind of initiation ceremony. They no doubt hoped that, in exchange for this show of pubescent bravado, they would be rewarded with some of Aigle's mighty strength.

The path bends to the right by the monument. A hundred yards further at a junction of paths bear to the left (5). Continue until reaching a gate on the edge of the moorland, at which point double back to the left along a grassy path with a wall on the right. Continue as the path descends into woodlands along the edge of Jack Flat. At a fork, bear to the right to descend to a stile to leave the woodlands. Shortly you will reach the A621 Sheffield Road (6). Cross to the stile on the opposite side of the road, to the left of the house.

Follow the clear path through the woodlands, going straight on at a crossroads as the path climbs gently uphill. Pass through a gap in a wall into a more open area surrounded by bracken. You are actually walking along the western edge of Gardom's Edge. The path re-enters woodland (7). Keep climbing and, at the top of the hill, pass through another gap in the wall. Ignore the left fork as you begin the descent to the A619. Climb over the wall stile onto the road (8), and turn left to return to Robin Hood which is the start/end of this walk.

The Robin Hood Public House

This would be an ideal time to relax and enjoy the hospitality of the Robin Hood Inn and as they say in many such establishments:

> *My beer is stout, my ale is good*
> *Pray stay and drink with Robin Hood*
> *If Robin Hood abroad has gone*
> *Pray stay and drink with Little John*
>
> *A glass of wine is sure to please*
> *Just one won't bring you to your knees*
> *There's tales of Robin and his crew*
> *His merry men and lasses too*

Walk 20: Robin Hood's Stride – Birchover – Winster

This walk begins at the old lead mining village of Winster and goes along part of the ancient Portway, a medieval trading route, to a rock outcrop known as Robin Hood's Stride. The two pinnacles that stand out against the sky lines are known to climbers as the Weasel and the Inaccessible, but according to legend Robin stepped from one to the other – thus the name. Not far from this is a small cave, undoubtedly a former hermitage because hewn in the rock is a crucifix some four feet high, a niche for a lamp, and a couch. According to records at Haddon Hall, it was occupied by a hermit who preached to travellers along

Winster was an important centre as this ancient stone stoop shows

Distance	3¾ miles (6km)
Starting point	Winster Market Hall
How to get there	From the A6 at Rowsley, take the B5056 until reaching the B5057 branching off to your left. Winster is reached in ½ mile
Parking	In the village street
Map	Ordnance Survey OS Explorer OL24
Map reference	GR 242605

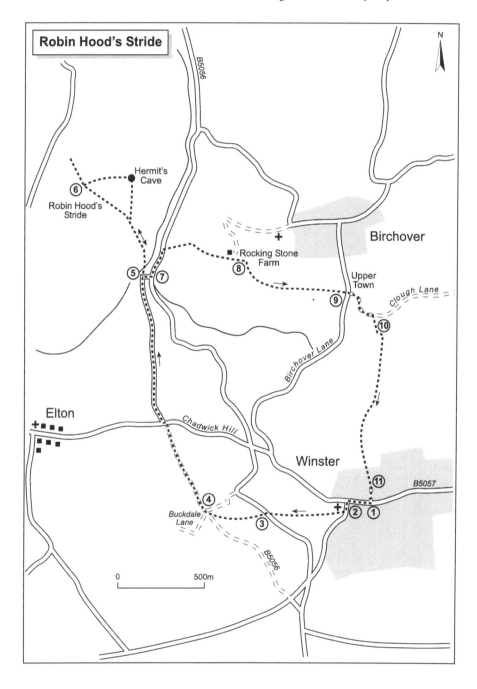

the Portway in the 16th century, although historians believe this was a much older practice.

The Robin Hood connection

This dramatic natural gritstone tor near Birchover is called Robin Hood's Stride, because in one easy stride Robin reputedly covered the 66ft (20 metres) distance between the two massive rock towers. In honour of this legendary feat, the outcrop has been known ever since as Robin Hood's Stride.

It would certainly have made a tremendous vantage point to view the area and watch for wealthy travellers along the Portway, the ancient route that dates back to Roman times and maybe even earlier. It's now a quiet track, but it would have been the motorway of its day.

The Walk

Our walk begins at Winster Market Hall (1).

Winster Market Hall

This 17th or early 18th century market hall was the first property in Derbyshire to be acquired by the National Trust, and now the restored building is a reminder of when cheese and cattle fairs were a prominent feature of local life.

With your back to the Market Hall, walk west along the main street, then turn left into West Bank (2). Almost at once, cross the road and go along a narrow alleyway which leads into the churchyard.

Keep left where the path forks, following the edge of the churchyard to a stile. Go through the stile into the parkland surrounding Oddo House. Follow the obvious path through several stiles. On a clear day it is possible to see the prominent outline of Robin Hood's stride and way beyond. When the road is reached (3), leave the parkland and cross with care. Go over a stile opposite and continue through fields. After the fourth stile the path bears right to a signposted stile where the route joins the medieval Portway (4). Turn right at the signpost and go straight on at the adjacent crossroads. An easy stroll along this green lane soon takes you to Elton Cross. When the Portway was the main road there was a pub here. Go across the road and down Dudwood Lane which descends steeply, soon passing the little hamlet of Dudwood (5). This is part of the Limestone Way.

At the bottom of the hill, go straight on, over a stile and up the broad track towards the rock formation shrouded in trees, known as Robin Hood's Stride. It's quite an invigorating upward tramp but the view from the summit is pretty remarkable.

I could see Robin making use of this elevated spot as a look out point, but the local legend tells of something much more worthy of note. Apparently Robin stood with one foot on each of the 'chimneys' and urinated into the valley below. Nine maidens passing were so shocked they were turned into stone.

From my elevated vantage point amongst the rocks and trees, I looked round for the nine stones hewn roughly into human form. I didn't expect to find any detail but I wanted to see standing stones or at least stones that had once stood. There weren't any. In a way I was pleased. After all, Robin Hood was a gentleman. He wouldn't have done that kind of thing – or would he? It's such a lonely spot, who would expect

The outline of Robin Hood's Stride silhouetted against the sky line

to find nine maidens passing just when you are answering a call of nature.

On leaving the Stride don't go back down the track, but instead go through the gate towards Cratcliffe Tor, which lies across a flat field in which are the remains of a palisaded encampment – well seen from the Stride. To the left can be seen the few remaining standing stones of Harthill Moor circle. At the far end of the field pass through a stile and turn right to locate the hermits cave.

Leave the cave by the steeply descending path, which soon reaches the edge of the wood at a stile. A path follows the edge of the wood back towards the Stride, but then goes left over a stile into the field. Follow the track back down the road to reach Dudwood Lane again.

Go left and left again at the B5056 main road (7), then walk for about 150 yards where just opposite a milepost, go right over a stile and back into fields.

A short, steep ascent takes you to a stile where you turn sharp right. Do not follow the more obvious track straight ahead. Almost at once bear left, following the wall beside the trees to another stile. An obvious path skirts the base of Rocking Stone Tor, passing the ruins of a barn, whose rear wall was hewn into a slab of rock. Pass Rocking Stone Farm on the left (8) and continue ahead with Birchover village now in view. Winster and Elton can be seen to the right across the valley.

The path keeps to the edge of the scarp, passing through a series of fields until the little settlement of Upper Town (9) is reached. Cross the road and go up the flight of steps opposite, passing through the yard of Cowley Knoll Farm to reach Clough Lane. Turn right here and follow the lane round the bend, where there is a great view across to Winster.

A little over 100 yards beyond the bend, go right at a footpath sign by a big ash tree (10). Follow the hedge on your right to a stile and gate, beyond which the land falls away steeply. Keep straight on with a little valley to the right, passing the end of a remnant hedge on the left until a broad path is reached. Follow this towards Winster. The path dips sharply to a stile, beyond which it becomes paved.

Follow this obvious route through a series of fields, gradually climbing towards the village. For the most part the stiles are obvious and way marked. Where the path joins a track (11), continue up hill, via the cattle grid, not the steps. The first houses of Winster on Woodhouse Lane are soon reached and the lane emerges in the main street close to the Market Hall which is the start/end of this walk.

Walk 21: Robin Hood's Mark and Ashover Butts

From the peaceful village of Ashover, nestling in the valley, this walk climbs up to Cocking Tor and the curious block of grit stone known as Robin Hood's Mark, from which are the most stunning views down over the valley. The name Ashover comes from the Saxon *Essovre*, meaning 'Beyond the Ash Trees', so it is not surprising to find that Ashover was mentioned in the 1086 Domesday Book.

Distance	3½ miles (5.65km)
Starting point	Ashover
How to get there	Take the A632 road that runs between Chesterfield and Matlock. At Kelstedge, take the B6036 sign posted to Ashover. Take the second turning on the left, Church Street and at the next junction, turn right. The car park is on your right
Parking	Car Park by the village hall and medical centre on Church Street
Map	Ordnance Survey OS Explorer OL269
Map reference	GR 350632

The Robin Hood connection

This is rather a mystery. There is no reason why this curious block of grit stone, which stands at over 900ft above sea level, was called Robin Hood's Mark. At one time it was noted as a rocking stone because it could be made to rock on its plinth with relative ease but, in the late 19th century, it was dislodged by some over enthusiastic rocking and it now rests solidly on its base. That's quite reassuring when the rock measures 26ft in circumference and has an estimated weight of 14 tons. From its lofty height it would have been a great look-out for the outlaw.

Our walk also includes the Butts, a name that probably dates from the 14th century when all able bodied men were expected to be proficient with the Longbow, ready to be called upon in case of a national disaster. By Royal decree, Sunday afternoons were set aside for archery practice in a designated area known as The Butts, named after the target used for shooting at.

The Walk

Leave the car park (1) and turn left towards the village, passing on your right The Black Swan, The Crispin and the church.

There are three very popular pubs in Ashover; The Poet's Corner, The Crispin and The Black Swan. The Black Swan was regularly featured in the TV series 'Peak Practice'. It's over 300 years old and the sport of bear baiting is said to have taken place in a large hollow behind the building. Named after the Patron saint of Cobblers and saddle makers, the Crispin was once a cobblers shop. Alternatively, it could have been named in recognition of the Battle of Agincourt fought on St Crispin's day on 25th October in 1415, as a thanks for the safe return of the Ashover men that fought in the battle and returned unscathed. The Crispin also took a prominent part in the Civil War, when the Royalists troops turned out the landlord and drank all the ale.

Ashover Parish Church was erected between 1350-1419, incorporating some earlier stonework. Inside the church is a Norman font dating from 1150 and made of stone covered in lead. It is extremely rare and only one of a handful in the country.

Continue down the hill to the junction of roads (2). Turn right along Butts road and, at the end of the row of houses on your left, take the track down the hill passing over the River Amber and the former track bed of the dismantled Ashover Light Railway (3).

Continue on the path up the hill and, after passing over a ruined stone wall, take a path climbing half up through the bushes. Near the top of the hill, look out for a wall of vertical stones slabs with a stile in them,

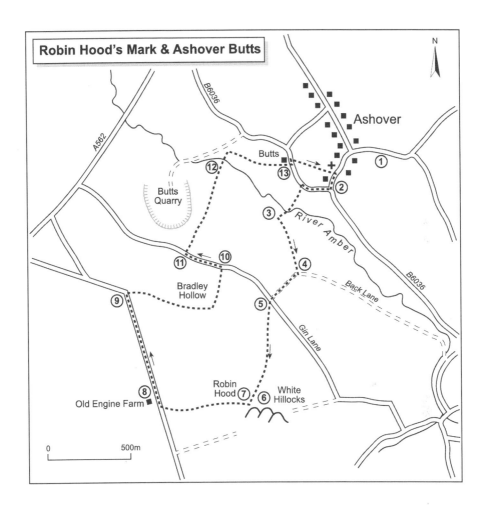

go through the stile and follow the right side of the next field to emerge onto a track, called Back Lane (4), through a squeeze stile. Turn left and follow Back Lane until meeting Gin Lane (5).

This is nothing to do with the colourless liquid that goes with tonic. This gin is short for engine, and was the name given to a primitive engine driven by horses, the type that would have been employed in the areas numerous mines. The area has a strong lead mining tradition and is rich in mineral deposits, particularly fluorspar and lead.

Cross Gin Lane and go straight ahead onto what becomes a flagged path, which continues through a wood. Emerging from the wood walk diagonally up and across an area called the White Hillocks (6).

These are spoil heaps from Gregory Mine, which were composed of sparkling white crystals of Calcite and Calc-spar. On a sunny day, their almost luminous whiteness was visible for miles around, but several periods of re-working for the mineral content has removed much of the sparkling material and the hillocks have now lost their lustre.

Follow the well trodden path past the old chimney down to your left and, when abreast of it, double back to the right towards the top of the workings, where the path enters woodland. The path climbs steeply but, just short of the top, meets another that runs along the ridge. This is Cocking Tor (7). To your right is Robin Hood's Mark, a curious block of grit stone which stands at over 900ft above sea level.

Nearby is another isolated outcrop of weathered grit stone, now almost submerged beneath a blanket of rhododendrons. Legend has it that this stone turns of its own accord when Ashover church clock strikes midnight.

The views down over Ashover in the valley

Retrace your steps along the ridge path, past the point of ascent and, almost immediately, turn left following a wall to a stone stile giving access to a field. Head for the edge of the Round Plantation to the front right. Walk to the bottom right hand corner of the field to a gate which opens onto Holestone Gate Road in front of Old Engine Farm (8). Turn right and walk along Holestone Gate Road enjoying the views over Riber on your left.

Where the road turns sharply left (9), take the sign posted footpath on the right and follow the path down through Bradley Hollow. On leaving the wood, follow the wall along the left hand side of the field and out onto the track before Greenend on Gin Lane (10). Turn left. Follow the road to Green House Farm on the left where on your right is a stile (11). Cross the stile and head towards the gates in front of you. Go through the right hand gate and, walking close to the wall on your left, look for a concrete stile at the top of the field. Go over the stile and head down into the bottom left hand corner of the field to a slip stile. Butts Quarry is over on your left.

Many towns and villages had places called Butts. Originally, they were the border lands that butted up to boundaries, then they became an area where archery practice was carried out, taking the name from the target.

Follow the boundary of the field for a short distance until reaching a stile on your right. Go through and head down a steep bank with steps heading for the River Amber (12). Cross at the stepping stones, and continue for a short distance until reaching another stile, in a wire fence, on your right. Go through, then cross Marsh Brook.

Head for a metal shed beneath the trees and cross the nearby stile to enter Butts Pasture. Head up to a stile with Butts Farm on your right and Butts Cottage on your left. Cross the stile onto a track that leads to Butts Road. Cross and veer left to a signed footpath between the houses. The path is between high hedges with stones stiles, then opens out with a stone wall on the right and Ashover School playing fields, wired off, on your left. The path reaches a short lane beside the churchyard, passing the converted old village bakehouse on the right to emerge on Church Street between The Chantry House and the churchyard. Turn left, passing The Crispin and the Black Swan to return to the car park which is the start/end of this walk.

Walk 22: Robin Hood – Crich and The Sherwood Foresters

Few people realise that there is a hamlet named Robin Hood between Whatstandwell and Gregory Tunnel in the parish of Crich. There are a few properties, a quarry and a former stone saw mill, built here because of the proximity of the quarry and to utilise the power of the stream that runs through the hamlet.

This is also one of the most picturesque sections of the Derwent Valley, unique in having three roads, the railway, the Cromford Canal and River Derwent all running parallel to each other through this narrow valley. Our walk begins in the valley and rises to Crich Stand, perched on the summit of the hill, in memory of the 11,409 Sherwood Foresters who died during the 1914-18 war.

The Robin Hood connection
Robin Hood is probably one of our best know freedom fighters but how many realise that his name continues in The Robin Hood Rifles, Nottinghamshire Army Cadet Force, a battalion of the Sherwood Foresters.

In *The Historical Record of the Royal Sherwood Foresters* by Captain AE Lawson, published in 1872, he wrote: 'At Agincourt in 1415, the Nottinghamshire Archers again played a prominent part, and there, for the first time on record, they fought as Sherwood Foresters'. Their banner was poetically described as:

> *'Old Nottingham – an archer clad in green,*
> *Under a tree with his drawn bow stood*
> *A chequered flag far off was seen;*
> *It was the picture of bold Robin Hood.'*

It would appear that Robin Hood was not only the first Sherwood Forester but has been the inspiration, and name given to millions of fighting men since. The Robin Hood Battalion saw action in France and Ireland during the first World War, and in 1921 the decision was

Distance	5 miles (8.10km)
Starting point	Whatstandwell
How to get there	Take the A6 Derby to Bakewell Road. Whatstandwell is just over 1¼ miles south of Cromford and 1¾ miles north of Ambergate. The Derwent Arms is on the bridge
Parking	The car park of the Derwent Arms with the landlord's permission if using the facilities or street parking nearby
Map	Ordnance Survey OS Explorer OL24 and OL269
Map reference	GR 332544

made to build and dedicate a tower at Crich as a memorial to the memory of the 11,409 Sherwood Foresters who had died during the war. This is now known as Crich Stand, and a regimental pilgrimage is held annually on the 1st Sunday in July

The Walk

Whatstandwell is sure to get people wandering where such a name sprang from.

According to historic records, a Wat (short for Walter) Standwell rented a cottage or 'held of the convent' on the site where the bridge was constructed in 1391. Prior to this people crossed the river at a ford, or they could have been ferried across by a boatman. Who would have been more handy than Wat Standwell? There's also a story that during the coaching era, part of the Derwent Arms was a toll bar and in the 1700s Walter Standwell used to be the tollmaster here. Yet, on Burdett's map of 1791, it is shown as 'Hottstandell Bridge', so the debate continues.

We start our walk at the 300 year old Derwent Arms Hotel (1) a former coaching inn known as The Bulls' Head where the Champion horse-

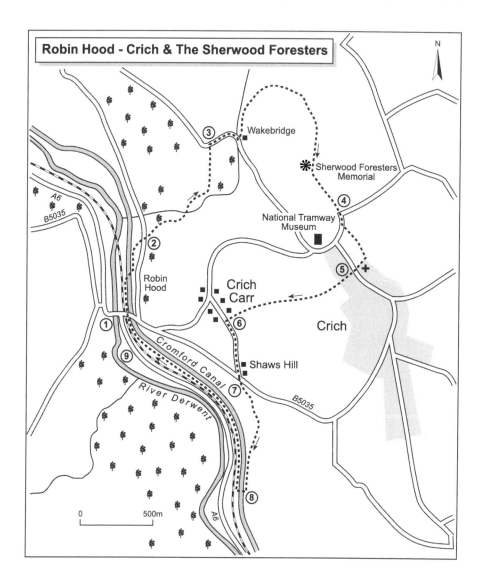

drawn coach would rest before tackling the steep hills out of the valley.

Whatstandwell is mentioned in the DH Lawrence novel 'Sons and Lovers', published in 1913, in a scene in which Paul Morel and Miriam go on a day's outing. "They went on, miles and miles, to Whatstandwell. All the food was eaten, everybody was hungry, and there was very little money to get home with. But they managed to procure a loaf and a currant-loaf, which they hacked to pieces with shut-knives, and ate sitting on a wall near the bridge, watching the bright Derwent rushing by, and the brakes from Matlock pulling up at the inn."

With the Derwent Arms Hotel (1) on your left, walk ahead up Main Road. After ascending for approximately 100 yards, turn left alongside the canal.

The Cromford canal, completed in 1794, was built to carry limestone from the quarries at Crich to the iron foundry at Butterley. It was extended to serve Richard Arkwright's Cromford Mills – the world's first successful water powered cotton spinning mills – and became very busy and profitable as a result. Today it supports an abundance of wildlife and has been designated a Site of Special Scientific Interest.

Walk by the canal for about 400 yards until reaching a footpath that takes you over the footbridge that crosses the canal. At the T-junction

Robin Hood Cottage in the hamlet of Robin Hood

of paths beyond, head away from the canal through the wood to the road (2). This is Robin Hood Road, and the hamlet of Robin Hood.

Robin Hood Road leads to Holloway and less than a mile up this road is Lea Hurst, once the home of Florence Nightingale, a name know throughout the world as the lady with the lamp.

Florence Nightingale was born in Florence in 1820, but it was here at Lea Hurst that Florence spent most of her life. She would have enjoyed a luxurious life style, financed by the income from local lead mining and industry, but Florence wanted more – she wanted to be a nurse, something that was totally unheard of for a woman of her station. It was the outbreak of the Crimean War that changed Florence's life for ever when, against much opposition, in October 1854 she set off with forty women to nurse the wounded at Scutari. It was thanks to her dedication that conditions improved and nursing became recognised as a respectable occupation.

When the war ended in 1856, Florence stayed behind until all the men were evacuated, refusing a passage for herself on a man-of-war, and the grand reception waiting for her back in England. Instead, registering as Miss Smith, she travelled on a small ship called the Danube and quietly made her way to London, then by train to Derbyshire. She arrived at Whatstandwell station, which was then at Whatstandwell Bridge, just behind the Derwent Hotel, then walked up Robin Hood Road to her family home at Lea Hurst.

Cross the road (2), following the track into the trees and ignoring a path a few yards later to the right. Subsequently ignore other paths to the right leading into the quarries. After crossing a bridge over a stream towards the end of the wood, ignore the stile to the left into the field. Carry straight on for 50 yards, climbing the stile into the field. Beyond this walk through a small wood, then wind through the first field after the wood, to reach a stile heading onto the road at Wakebridge (3). Turn right, then after 20 yards turn left up the track to Straddlestone. Stay on this track walking towards Cliff Farm ahead.

Lead mining has been carried out in this area since pre-Roman days, and there have been many Roman coins of copper and silver found, especially around Crich Hill.

Take the path to the right 50 yards before the farmhouse. Follow this as it ascends, ignoring a path to the left. You may see trams from the Tramway Museum above to the right. Bear right and cross the tramline.

Crich Tramway Museum houses an amazing collection of transport memorabilia and interesting trams, many of which are in working order, and give rides to visitors along the section of woodland track you are now walking.

Proceed up the gravel track, following the line of electricity poles. Where the path splits, bear right slightly uphill.

In 1734 there were a number of small lime kilns on Crich Hill and the public footpath, which runs across to Crich, is believed to have been used by salt merchants who packed the salt on horses or mules transporting it southward from the Cheshire area .

Stay with the path, which leads you towards Crich Stand, the memorial to the Sherwood Foresters.

It is usually open and there is a box for collecting a small entrance fee. Climb the steps, are there 57 or 58? On a clear day the view from here is superb and it's reckoned that more people are born within sight of Crich Stand than any other Derbyshire building.

Crich Stand built in memory to the Sherwood Foresters

The name Crich simply means 'hill', an apt name when it's 995ft above sea level. The summit was probably the site of an early cairn or burial chamber. It's reputed to have been the site of a Beacon fire signalling the sighting of the Spanish Armada in the English Channel in 1588.

Robin was the first Sherwood Forester, here depicted with a later recruit, in a picture in Mansfield stone, built into a wall at Bestwood Lodge Hotel

A wooden tower was erected to mark the ascension of George III, in 1769, but that was replaced, in 1788, with a conical limestone tower, which fell down. In 1849, a third tower was built but it was not a case of third time lucky! In June 1882, there was a major landslide in the nearby quarry and the tower suffered from subsidence. Things seemed to remain static for the next 30 years, then three years after the end of the first World War, the tower was dismantled and re-built close by in more or less the same form and dedicated to the Sherwood Foresters.

Leaving the Stand, walk towards the village of Crich and, at the road (4), bear right round the corner. Just before the low stone outbuilding on the left, pass through a stile at the side of a gate. Walk in the general direction of the church, staying on the right side of the fields ahead. Pass through the kissing gate beside the old barn and enter the churchyard. Bear right and walk round to the front of the church.

St Mary's Church, Crich was consecrated in 1135. The chancel, aisle, tower and spire were all rebuilt in the 14th century when the nave was lengthened but it's quite daunting to think that the Norman arcades to the nave and a massive circular Norman font were around in Robin Hood's time.

From the church porch, go to the gate and cross the road (5).

Crich was turned into the fictional village of Cardale in the ITV medical drama 'Peak Practice' which ran from 1992-2002. Wirksworth writer

St Mary's Church, Crich

Lucy Gannon had the initial idea and wrote the first episodes of 'Peak Practice', which was filmed all around this area. Now an estimated 2.6 million visitors go to Crich to look at places like the Cardale Chippy, Allsop's bakery and Archway House which was Dr Beth Glover's (Amanda Burton) house in the series. Although Crich formed the backdrop for village life many actual sites were outside the village.

Turn left then, almost immediately, right to descend Dowie Way, ignoring Hodder Close to the left. After 40 yards, bear left over the stone bridge. Carry straight on in the field beyond. Just after halfway along the wall side, pass through the stile at the gateway on your right, then go immediately left up the wall side. Head slightly away from the wall towards the gap stile ahead between the two gateways. Proceed towards the next stile in front, walking down the right side of the next field. There's a wide view of the surrounding countryside in front. Walk down the left side of the following field. Keep straight on in the next but stay to the right of the buildings of Benthill Farm. Descend along the path then down the steps to the road below (6).

We are now back in Whatstandwell in the middle of land-locked Derbyshire, so who would have believed that a child growing up here could become the fastest woman to sail round the world single-handed. That's the achievement of Dame Ellen MacArthur, a 26 year old, 5ft slip of girl, who beat all her male counterparts, broke records and made headlines all over the world. She's been named Yaughtsman of the Year, and voted second in the BBC Sports Personality of the Year 2001, an incredible achievement considering the awards are usually dominated by mainstream sports. Ellen MacArthur is an inspirational personality for thousands around the world and we're proud to say she's a Derbyshire girl.

Turn left before descending Shaws Hill to the B5035 road (7). The views are splendid and there's a seat to sit and enjoy them, then walk down the track to the left of the seat. Stay on this path, ignoring all paths off and descend to the Cromford canal (8). Cross the bridge over the canal before turning right on the far side. Walk along the tow-path with the canal on your right for a mile until passing under the footbridge near Whatstandwell railway station (9).

The Manchester, Buxton, Matlock and Midlands Junction Railway was opened in 1849 to serve the village and is now operated by East Midland trains. As mentioned previously, the first station was replaced by this station in 1894.

Continue until reaching the stone road bridge at Whatstandwell and turn left down the road to return to the Derwent Hotel which is the start/end of this walk.

Walk 23: The Hamlet of Robin Hood – Cromford Canal and Duke's Quarry

Another delightful walk through the hamlet of Robin Hood.

The Robin Hood connection
Few people realise that this charming little hamlet between Whatstandwell and Holloway exists, so we could say this is a Robin Hood secret.

The Walk

Our walk begins in the lay-by near Wakebridge Farm, Crich (1). Go through a tubular iron gate at a footpath sign on the left and walk half right across the field until a disused barn comes into view. Head for the barn, but change directions just before reaching it. Turn right

Distance	2½ miles (4km)
Starting point	Wakebridge
How to get there	Leave the A6 at Whatstandwell, go up the hill on the B5035, then turn left just past the Crich Carr Church of England School, into Hindersitch Lane, which becomes Coddington Lane, just before entering Crich. At the junction turn left alongside the perimeter of the Crich Tramway Village
Parking	The lay-by near Wakebridge Farm
Map	Ordnance Survey OS Explorer OL24 and OL269
Map reference	GR 342553

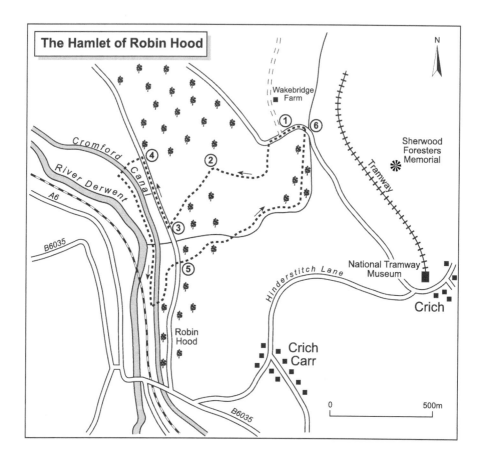

The Hamlet of Robin Hood

down a depression which runs along the hillside. This leads to a stile at a blocked off gateway. In the next field, go half left towards the crest of a hillock until a wooden fence is seen ahead. The path follows this fence down to a gate, but why not take a short detour to the top of the knoll just to your right (2).

This is an idea vantage point to view the surrounding countryside. On the extreme right is Holloway, nestling in the hillside. Let your eye travel to the left and you will see Lea Hurst, Florence Nightingale's former home, the entrance to Gregory tunnel on the Cromford Canal, the river Derwent in close proximity to the railway and the A6 trunk road. Closer is the small cluster of houses at Robin Hood and further round to our left are the farms at Alderwasley. It's a truly magnificent panorama.

To return to our walk. Follow the wooden fence and go through the gate to continue along the bridle path down to the road at the group of cottages known as Robin Hood (3). One serves refreshment so why not pause a while.

Leave Robin Hood and turn right to walk up the road. Where two gateways face each other across the road, turn left into the driveway of Leashaw Farm (4). After crossing the canal bridge and entering the farmyard, turn immediately through a stone stile which is built into the bridge. This brings us onto the tow-path of the canal. With the canal on our left and the River Dewent on our right, continue until reaching a modern

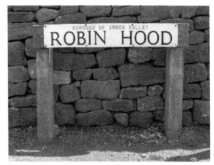

Robin Hood in the Borough of Amber Valley

footbridge which spans the canal. Here, leave the tow path and cross the canal to the woodland on the opposite bank. Continue ahead to reach Robin Hood Road (5). Cross over to a continuation of the path on the opposite side of the road. This leads through a secluded, almost secret area of deserted quarries known as Duke's Quarries.

Keep to the main path (unless you want to explore), passing through unspoilt meadows until emerging back on the main road at Wakebridge (6) through a stone stile, which in summer is patrolled by wood ants. Turn right to reach the lay-by which is the start/end of this walk.

Walk 24:
Bolsover Castle

Not many buildings in Britain occupy such a splendid position as Bolsover's fairy tale castle, perched on the brow of a limestone ridge above the valley of the River Rother. A great example of Jacobean Romantic Architecture, standing almost chateau-like, this little castle evokes thoughts of medieval castles and pageantry. It's therefore not surprising to find that a castle has stood here since at least the 12th century.

Bolsover Castle passed through a variety of owners until it was sold to Sir Charles Cavendish, son of Bess of Hardwick on August 19th 1613. When he died, his son William continued the work. It was during

Distance	5 miles (8.10km)
Starting point	Bolsover
How to get there	The direction signs from the M1 take the driver off at junction 29A, the new one which is 2 miles from Bolsover. Follow the signs along Markham Lane through the M1 Commerce Park until reaching a round-about and the A623. Take the second turning off the roundabout and head towards Bolsover. Go up the hill and take the first turn off to your right. This is Castle Street and the car park is on your left
Parking	Our walk begins at the car park on Castle Street, Bolsover
Map	Ordnance Survey OS Explorer OL269
Map reference	GR 472705

Bolsover's impressive castle might have been built at Nottingham

this time that Sir William Cavendish purchased Nottingham Castle, a broken down, burnt out shell, and proceeded to build the Palladian style structure we see there today. But just imagine what would have happened if the designs had been changed over. Bolsover Castle with its impressive Keep might have dominated the skyline of Nottingham, and Nottingham's Palladian style citadel could have been sited on the high Derbyshire ridge at Bolsover.

The Robin Hood connection

Before the Norman conquest, in 1066, when Bolsover was in the Saxon kingdom of Mercia, William the Conqueror granted the manor and one hundred and sixty one others to his illegitimate son William Peveril who was also put in charge of the Royal Forest of Sherwood. The first written mention of Sherwood Forest, in 1154, states 'William Peverill in the first year of Henry I answers to the Pleas of the Forest 3'.

As with Peveril Castle at Castleton, in the first rush of castle building after 1066, William Peveril would have built a rudimentary castle at

Its highly likely that Robin would have been familiar with Bolsover Castle

Bolsover as part of the fortification of the rocky ridge. A succession of Peverils, who all seem to have had the name William, would have had the whole profit and command of Sherwood Forest. The Peverils then went out of favour when they backed the wrong side against the new King Henry II, in 1152. After this, the Royal Forest of Sherwood devolved to the Crown and was managed by The High Sheriff of Nottingham and Derbyshire. This would account for why there was hostility between Robin Hood and the sheriff, yet no tales of friction between Robin Hood and the Peverils.

The Peveril's castles would then be held by the King and run by a constable appointed by him. In 1173, it is recorded that a joint sum of £135 was spent on knights and their servants at Bolsover, Peveril and Nottingham Castles. Amongst other duties, these knights would have been employed to transport the King's taxes and to capture Robin Hood.

It's highly likely that Robin was familiar with Bolsover and its castle, damaged during a siege, which was part of the baron's revolt against King John. Gerald de Furnival defended the castle for the King, while William de Ferrars, 4th Earl of Derby, attacked for the barons. Yet William de Ferrars (1168-1247) stood surety for King John on 13th May, 1213. He was loyal to both Richard I and his treacherous brother John.

But there is an even closer link to Robin Hood. William, Earl of Ferrars was one of the party chosen by King Richard to travel with him when, disguised as monks, they set off into the greenwood to encounter Robin Hood.

The Walk

Leave the car park (1), and turn into High Street, passing the Blue Bell Inn on your right and the Parish Church on your left. At the road junction, where High Street meets the A632 Langwith Road, go straight ahead passing the town's earthwork on your left. The road curves round to the left and on the right of the bend is the path you will be returning on from Palterton. This area is Hillstown.

Continue round the bend and turn right into the Mansfield Road (2). In a few yards we will pass the West View Hotel, on the left and, at the footpath sign (3), leave the road and cross the playing fields with the Ace of Clubs on your left. Aim for the far right hand corner of the first field, then continue through the fields towards Scarcliffe. In about ½ mile, as you approach a flat mound, keep to the left of it, and continue across two stiled fields until arriving at the B6417 Rotherham Road. Cross over to the minor road (4) and follow this into Scarcliffe.

At the junction with the Main Street, turn left. Near the telephone kiosk on your right is Gang Lane which you will be taking, but you might first like to visit Scarcliffe Church, so continue down the Main Street and St Leonard's church is on your left (5).

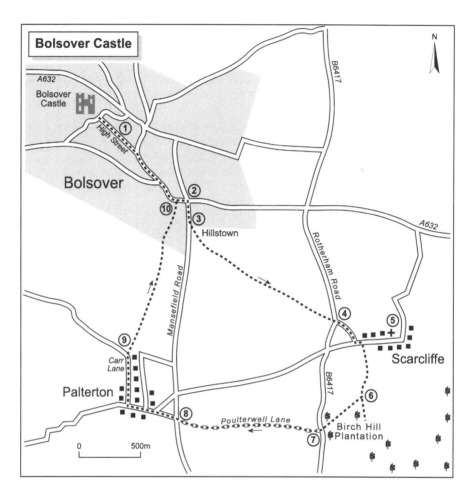

Inside St Leonard's church, Scarcliffe is an alabaster monument to Lady Constantia de Frecheville showing her plaited hair neatly coiled and surmounted by a coronet. Her right hand is folded across her chest and her left hand holds a baby, whose tiny hand is reaching up to the lady's face. It is eight hundred years old yet tells a poignant story as old as time.

The family de Frenchville held Scarcliffe Manor in the thirteenth century at a time when many men went off to fight the war in the Holy Land, in support of King Richard. It is highly probable that Lady

Constantia's lover had gone off to the Crusades leaving her unknowingly to suffer the ignominity of bearing a bastard child alone. In desperation, she decided to leave her home taking the much loved baby, and headed for the thicket of Scarcliffe Wood. It was probably her intention to never return yet, as she heard the curfew bell tolling, she felt it was calling her back to Scarcliffe and guiding her safely home.

The ancient tomb of
Lady Constantia

When she died, in gratitude she left five acres of land to pay for the ringing of the curfew bell. Her bequest is mentioned on a fixed slab, dated 1832, above her ancient tomb by the wall in the south aisle of the church. The custom of ringing the evening curfew bell at Scarcliffe continues for three weeks before and three weeks after Christmas in memory of Lady Constantia.*

Return to Gang Lane and follow the track for ¼ mile until reaching the last field before Birch Hill Plantation (6). Turn right through a stile and cross the field towards its far right hand corner, where a gap in the perimeter wall of the plantation gives access to a footpath. Follow this round to your right to a wider path and follow the footpath signs until reaching Mansfield Road (7).

Cross the road and go along the bridle path opposite – Poulterwell Lane which you will follow due west for ½ mile to the road junction on the eastern side of Palterton (8). Cross the road and walk along Main Street towards Palterton.

Continue to the edge of the vale and turn right, still following the road. This is Carr Lane. Walk to the end, where it swings down to the left, then leave the road to pass between the buildings of The Elms Farm (9) straight ahead. Follow the well defined path along the summit of the vale until reaching the aptly named Hillstown. Pass the houses until reaching the A632 Langwith Road (10). Now you will retrace your steps, turning into the High Street, but instead of returning to the car park, which is on your right, turn left into Castle Lane and the castle entrance is ahead.

Also from Sigma Leisure:

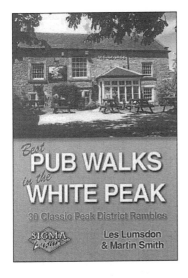

Best Pub Walks in the White Peak
30 Classic Peak District Rambles
Les Lumsden & Martin Smith

The 30 fabulous walks range from three to nine miles and ideal for family rambles. They start in such delightful Peak District villages as Ashford-in-the-Water, Alstonefield and Youlgreave, most of which are accessible by public transport — so that you can leave the car at home and savour the products on offer at the authors' favourite pubs.

Follow the recommendatios in this well-established — and completely updated — book for a superb variety of walks in splendid scenery and, after each walk, relax in a Peak District pub renowned for its welcome to walkers and for the quality of its Real Ale, often supplied by local independent brewers.

£7.95

Peak District Walking
On The Level
Norman Buckley

Some folk prefer easy walks, and sometimes there's just not time for an all-day yomp. In either case, this is definitely a book to keep on your bookshelf. Norman Buckley has had considerable success with "On The Level" books for the Lake District and the Yorkshire Dales.

The walks are ideal for family outings and the precise instructions ensure that there's little chance of losing your way. Well-produced maps encourage everybody to try out the walks - all of which are well scattered across the Peak District.

£7.95

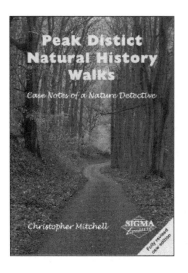

Peak District Walking Natural History Walks

Christopher Mitchell

An updated 2nd Edition with 18 varied walks for all lovers of the great outdoors — and armchair ramblers too! Learn how to be a nature detective, a 'case notes' approach shows you what clues to look for and how to solve them. Detailed maps include animal tracks and signs, landscape features and everything you need for the perfect natural history walk. There are mysteries and puzzles to solve to add more fun for family walks — solutions supplied! Includes follow on material with an extensive Bibliography and 'Taking it Further' sections.

£8.99

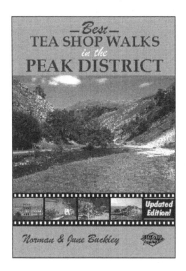

Best Tea Shop Walks in the Peak District

Norman and June Buckley

A wonderful collection of easy-going walks that are ideal for families and all those who appreciate fine scenery with a touch of decandence in the shape of an afternoon tea or morning coffee —or both! The 26 walks are spread widely across the Peak District, including Lyme Park, Castleton, Miller's Dale, and The Roaches and — of course — such famous dales as Lathkill and Dovedale. Each walk has a handy summary so that you can choose the walks that are ideally suited to the interests and abilities of your party. The tea shops are just as diverse, ranging from the splendour of Chatsworth House to more basic locations. Each one welcomes ramblers and there is always a good choice of tempting goodies.

£7.95

Derbyshire Walks with Children
William D Parke

There are 24 circular walks, ranging from 1 to 6 miles in length, and each one has been researched and written with children in mind. The directions and background information have been checked and revised as necessary for this updated reprint.

Detailed instructions for parents and an interactive commentary for children mean there's never a dull moment. There are even 'escape routes' to allow families to tailor each walk to suit their own needs, time and energy.

"The needs, entertainment and safety of children have been of paramount importance."
– Peak Advertiser
£8.99

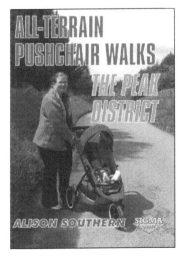

All-Terrain Pushchair Walks: The Peak District
Alison Southern

The Peak District, in the heart of the country, has some of England's most picturesque landscapes, from the White Peak in the south with its rocky outcrops and steep hills, to the Dark Peak in the north with peat moss moorland and stunning vistas. This book is for families with all-terrain pushchairs and buggies, and for everyone wishing to avoid as many stiles and obstacles as possible. Includes family-friendly attractions, trees to identify, birds and plants to spot, and lots more to discover. Have fun while you walk enjoying the amazing views, have some healthy exercise and spend time with the family away from the modern world.
£7.95.

Peak District Trigpointing Walks
Hill walking with a point to it!
Keith Stevens & Peter Whittaker

A superb introduction to an intriguing new walking experience: searching out all those elusive Ordnance Survey pillars. Packed with detailed walks to new and interesting Peak District summits, with a wealth of fascinating information on the history of the OS and the art of GPS navigation.

There are 150 Peak District Ordnance Survey pillars — can you find them all? Walk to all the best scenic viewpoints — from the top you can spot all the surrounding pillars. This book shows you how.
£8.95

Walks in the Ancient Peak District
Robert Harris

A collection of walks visiting the prehistoric monuments and sites of the Peak District. A refreshing insight into the thinking behind the monuments, the rituals and strange behaviour of our ancestors. All the routes are circular, most starting and finishing in a town or village that is easy to locate and convenient to reach by car.
£8.99

All of our books are all available through booksellers. For a free catalogue, please contact:

**SIGMA LEISURE, STOBART HOUSE, PONTYCLERC, PENYBANC ROAD
AMMANFORD, CARMARTHENSHIRE SA18 3HP
Tel: 01269 593100   Fax: 01269 596116**

info@sigmapress.co.uk   www.sigmapress.co.uk